Praise for Pat Conroy's
A LOWCOUNTRY HEART

"Resplendent . . . As always, [Conroy's] storytelling, word choice and rhythm are gorgeous, almost lyrical; his descriptions are gloriously unexpected. . . . Fans who have missed his voice will find comfort in knowing that [this] is distinctively, precisely, willfully the Conroy whose books they loved." —*USA Today*

"Elegant . . . *A Lowcountry Heart* is Pat's last offering—a victory lap for the legion of readers who bought his books and stood in line to get them signed. It will not disappoint." —*The Washington Post*

"*A Lowcountry Heart* is a fascinating look into the mind of one of the South's greatest authors; call it a secret glimpse at the person behind the pen with all his foibles and endearing qualities laid bare by his own hand. Funny, thoughtful, breezy, profound, in this posthumous account, he and his widow give readers a great gift: himself, something to remember him by and cherish for years to come." —Jackson *Clarion-Ledger*

"Fans of Conroy . . . will relish the chance to spend more time with him in this glowing valedictory to his life and writing. . . . Vibrant, charming . . . eloquent, folksy, and sometimes brutally honest." —*Publishers Weekly*

BY PAT CONROY

The Boo

The Water Is Wide

The Great Santini

The Lords of Discipline

The Prince of Tides

Beach Music

My Losing Season

The Pat Conroy Cookbook: Recipes of My Life

South of Broad

My Reading Life

The Death of Santini

A Lowcountry Heart

A

LOWCOUNTRY
HEART

PAT CONROY

A
LOWCOUNTRY
HEART

REFLECTIONS ON A
WRITING LIFE

THE DIAL PRESS

NEW YORK

2017 Dial Press Trade Paperback Edition

Published in the United States by The Dial Press,
an imprint of Random House, a division of
Penguin Random House LLC, New York.

THE DIAL PRESS and the HOUSE colophon are registered
trademarks of Penguin Random House LLC.

Originally published in hardcover in the United States
by Nan A. Talese / Doubleday, a division of
Penguin Random House LLC, in 2016.

LIBRARY OF CONGRESS CATALOGING-IN-PUBLICATION DATA
Names: Conroy, Pat.
Title: A lowcountry heart: reflections on a writing life / Pat Conroy.
Description: New York : Nan A. Talese, 2016
Identifiers: LCCN 2016026695 (print) | LCCN 2016036633 (ebook) |
ISBN 9780385343534 (paperback) | ISBN 9780385530873 (ebook)
Subjects: LCSH: Conroy, Pat. | BISAC: LITERARY
COLLECTIONS / Essays. | LITERARY COLLECTIONS / Letters.
Classification: LCC PS3553.05198 A6 2016 (print) |
LCC PS3553.05198 (ebook) | DDC 813/ .54 [B] —DC23
LC record available at https://lccn.loc.gov/2016026695

Printed in the United States of America on acid-free paper

randomhousebooks.com

2 4 6 8 9 7 5 3 1

*This book is dedicated with
great love and gratitude to Pat Conroy's
devoted readers.*

Contents

||||||||||||

A Note to the Reader, by Nan A. Talese | *XIII*

Introduction, by Cassandra King | *1*

✯ *HEY, OUT THERE* ✯

The First Letter: An Opening to the Light | *15*

Surprises on the Road | *20*

The Fire Sermon: Speech by Pat Conroy,
Delivered at Penn Center | *28*

On the Future of Books | *35*

My Spooky Life | *38*

CONTENTS

My Blogging Life | 42

The Boo's Lambs Gather in Charleston | 45

Hitch 22: A Great Memoir | 55

The Night the Band Played the "Tennessee Waltz" | 59

The Man Who Inspired *My Losing Season* Left Us
Too Soon . . . | 67

A Room of Her Own . . . and the Birth of *Moonrise* | 74

On the Road Again . . . Airports, Editors, Publicists,
and My Writing Life | 79

A Long-Lasting Friendship: Charlie Gibson of
Good Morning America | 84

Vietnam Still Haunting Me . . . | 89

The Teachers of My Life | 95

Barbara Warley Was Loved by Everyone | 105

How George R. R. Martin Made Me Love Dire Wolves,
Giants, Dwarves, and Dragons . . . | 113

A Eulogy for a Southern Gentleman | 131

Remembering an Irreplaceable Friend | 140

CONTENTS

The Best Night in the Life of This Aging Citadel
Point Guard . . . | 160

The Summer I Met My First Great Man | 169

Andie MacDowell at the Beaufort Film Festival | 174

Mina & Conroy Fitness Studio | 178

A Few Things I Wish I Had Told Ann Patchett . . . | 189

Conroy at Seventy—Happy Birthday to Me | 199

On Pat Conroy's Facebook Page on the Day of His
Passing | 209

⤚ *THE GREAT CONROY* ⤙

A Conversation with Pat Conroy | 213

A Letter to My Grandson on Sportsmanship and
Basketball | 222

Pat Conroy Talks About the South, His Mother, and
The Prince of Tides | 227

Pat Conroy Speaks to Meredith Maran | 231

On My Paris Days | 241

CONTENTS

A Letter to the Editor of the *Charleston Gazette* | 254

A Lowcountry Heart | 259

Pat Conroy's Citadel Speech | 262

Farewell Letter, by Bernie Schein | 275

The Great Conroy: An Homage to a Southern Literary
Giant and a Prince of a Guy, by Rick Bragg | 283

Eulogy, Delivered by Judge Alex Sanders | 287

Acknowledgments, by Cassandra King | 297

A Note to the Reader

||||||||||||||

When Pat Conroy died, we all felt bereft. He had sent me less than two hundred pages of his new novel, *The Storms of Aquarius*, about four male friends and teachers who came of age during the Vietnam War years, which he very much wanted to finish, but that was not to be. We are still searching his journals for more on this novel, and at some point we may have something to share with you. However, because we did not want his faithful readers to be without something from him, we gathered together his "blogs" (he hated the word), some letters and essays he would have wanted to share with you, and an interview, and we asked his wife, Cassandra King, who is also a writer, to contribute an introduction. Additionally, we included the farewell letter from his best and oldest friend, Bernie Schein. What follows is all of this, under the title *A Lowcountry Heart*.

—Nan A. Talese
   Editor

A

LOWCOUNTRY

HEART

Introduction

||||||||||||||

Pat Conroy and I met in 1995, several months before his fiftieth birthday. Being a year older than he was, I had already passed that milestone. Pat would later write that he never imagined a man and woman in their fifties could fall in love and build a happy, prolific life together. In our youth-obsessed society, we are conditioned to believe that our best years are behind us. Instead, Pat and I found that our fifties and sixties were a time of great joy, productivity, and contentment. We were looking forward to sharing our seventies together, with new books under way and at least a couple more waiting in the wings. After an exhausting but exhilarating weekend-long festival celebrating Pat's seventieth birthday in

October of 2015, he settled down to finish the new novel he had started. Life was good.

Pat was always happiest when he was writing, when he lost himself in the narrative that overtook him and flowed from his pen onto the pages of the yellow legal pads he used for his books. His musings, critiques, observations, and meditations he was more likely to write in his journals, which are also full of bits and pieces of stories he hoped to use one day. Pat collected stories like others might collect rare stamps, or a library of illustrious music. Hearing a good story filled him with great excitement. Afterward, he was apt to grab a pen and say to the teller, "Consider that story stolen. If you plan to write it one day, you'd better do it first."

Story was the way Pat connected with his readers. They couldn't seem to get enough of his stories, nor could he get enough of theirs. His readers wrote him long, heartrending letters about how they related to his writings, and the various ways his life story paralleled and validated theirs. He read them all, and would have answered each letter had he been able to do so. For a long time, Pat resisted and scorned modern technology, with its e-mails and blogs and tweets and twitters. Only when he realized that he could connect with more of his readers through the marvel of technology did he give in. Most of the works in this collection come from the blog he began to write when he was between books, when his health began to fail and he couldn't travel as much. He called his blog posts "letters," and came to embrace them as what he called "a nightmare for someone who never learned to type, and in other ways an opening to the light."

The "light" Pat was referring to was his bread and butter, the connection he made with others that brought him not only such great joy, but also such great material. It was the way he collected the stories he would turn into the books that his readers clamored for, the ones that mirrored their own experiences and gave them a voice for the first time in their lives. It was Pat's winning ways that made the connection happen. His interest in everyone he met was palpable, so intense that it was impossible to resist. I should know; I experienced it the first time I met him, at a writers' conference in Birmingham, Alabama. Before I knew what was happening, I had fallen under his spell, as I was to witness so many others do in the years to come.

When our first meeting was over, Pat Conroy knew a lot more about me than I ever intended to tell him.

I'm notoriously closemouthed and private; so much so that he would later nickname me Helen Keller. Not only were Helen Keller and I both native Alabamians, he said, but like my namesake, I saw nothing, heard nothing, said nothing. I would also learn that this was typical Conroy humor, though I didn't think it funny at the time. Pat could make the deaf hear and the mute speak. Sweeping you up in a conversation, with those intense blue eyes focused like lasers on you and you alone, he had the ability to ferret out your secret self that had been undercover for a lifetime. Before you realized what had happened, you had confided in him, told him about the past no one else knew about, the stories no one had heard before, the skeletons locked away in the family closet.

In my and Pat's almost twenty years together, I saw the same thing happen a million times. Starstruck, people approached their favorite writer in awe, rendered speechless by his presence. I can't tell you the number of times I've seen someone burst into tears on meeting him. The comment I've heard most frequently since Pat's been gone is "How could this be? He was larger than life." I've said it myself, a dozen times. Someone wrote that Pat didn't fill up a room when he entered it, he *was* the room. Yes! That was

Pat, the night we met. A previous commitment had made me run late and almost miss meeting him, then I'd made a fool of myself by blurting out something stupid when we were introduced. Before long, he'd forced me to confess that yes, I had a book coming out soon. I also confessed that I lacked the confidence to call myself a writer. Pat was the one who did that. "What do you mean, you're not *really* a writer?" he said in exasperation. "You have a book coming out. You wrote it. You're a writer. Got it?" When I muttered that it was just a little book, or something equally inane, he brushed me off. "Have your publisher send it to me, and if I like it, I'll give you a blurb. If not, I'll pretend it got lost in the mail."

Over the years, I would think about our first meeting as I watched Pat at signings for the five books he wrote in our time together. It was a sight to behold. Once, during an interview with the two of us, I said that Pat was extremely outgoing. Pat was quick to correct me. "I'm obnoxiously friendly," he told the reporter. "It's pathetic, actually." He went on to illustrate in more detail. "I was showing my former father-in-law around Fripp Island several years ago, and I waved and spoke to everyone we saw. Finally my father-in-law, who was a New Yorker, said, 'What's going on? You running for mayor or something?'" It became a buzzword with us. After one of Pat's endless conversations with a waiter, taxi driver, flight attendant, hotel maid, or bellhop, I'd lean over and whisper, "Hey, you running for mayor or something?"

But book signings were something else altogether. After attending a couple of them when we were newly married and I didn't know any better, I learned not to tag along unless I was prepared for anywhere from five to eight hours' wait. Foolishly, I'd thought if I were there, I could make Pat—who was diabetic, prone to crippling hand cramps and severe back pain—take a break. No one could sit for that many hours without a bathroom break, could they? The only time I ever signed for eight hours, my hands were shaking so badly before it was over that I couldn't hold a pen, and I'd not only taken several trips to the bathroom but also downed endless glasses of sweet tea for low blood sugar. How on earth did Pat do it?

Pat's book signings told me everything I ever needed to know about him. He refused to take even the quickest of breaks. The staff and I would plead with him, but to no avail. I'd insist the staff have food for him, which they probably loved me for, since they'd end up eating it. He certainly didn't. He would sign until the last person left, even if it was well after midnight. He greeted everyone as though he were running for mayor. He was known for shaking off the efforts of his publicist to hurry the line along, or to stop anyone from bringing more than one book to be signed. "Bring all you have!" Pat would tell his readers jovially, much to the chagrin of the poor publisher's representatives who had been sent to make sure everything went smoothly. I'd see them glare daggers at him at first, but learned quickly to quell my alarm. In no time, I knew, the silver-tongued devil would have them eating out of his hand. And without fail, he always did. Despite the long, exhausting hours and doubtless unpaid overtime Pat's signings cost the staff, it was a sheer pleasure to be with him when he arrived at a bookstore. He was always greeted like visiting royalty, and knew each of the staff by name. He asked after their families, and if they'd ever gotten around to writing the book they had told him about, the last time he was in. Never mind that it had been many years since his last signing there. He remembered everyone.

But more than anything else, Pat's signings were lovefests between him and his readers, and they flocked to him. He made sure their long wait was worth it. Once they got to his table, he'd hold out his hand and say, "Hi, I'm Pat Conroy. Tell me who you are." In no time, he had pried their stories from them, just as he'd done with me the night we met. Devoted readers would burst into tears upon meeting him, then end up blurting out their innermost secrets, not caring how long they held up the line. It was another thing I observed with amusement, the disgruntled moans and groans of those in line when someone was taking up what appeared to be way too much of Mr. Conroy's time. What was *wrong* with the staff, that they allowed such a thing to happen? Didn't that fancy New York publicist know he/she was supposed to be herding the crowd along and not just standing there mesmerized? Couldn't *someone* do *something*? They would fume and pout until their time came, and then—like magic—it would all disappear. I would watch them melt under Pat's twinkly-eyed gaze, his disarming smile and outstretched hand. Next thing you knew, they too would be leaning over the table, telling him in a low breathless voice a story they'd never, ever told anyone before. No wonder he never ran out of material.

Tragically, Pat Conroy ran out of time before he ran out of material, and it breaks my heart to think of the stories he did not live to tell. He and I talked often of Time's winged chariot drawing near, and how swiftly it all goes by. Although Pat feared little, one fear haunted him: that he'd run out of time before he could finish the books he still had in him. It was almost a premonition. He was a man who loved the written word beyond all measure, and who believed that each of us has at least one great story to tell. He would grab hold of someone—stranger or friend, it didn't matter—and he wouldn't let go until he pried that story out. Then his eyes would blaze that dazzling Irish blue and a smile would transform him. If the story was good enough to capture his imagination, he couldn't wait to write it down. Whether it was about a white porpoise or a caged tiger or a lost ancestor who sewed coins into the hem of a skirt to buy her freedom, his pen would bring it to life, make it as real to the rest of us as it was to him on hearing it. He would take your story and make it large and glorious and unforgettable. He would make it immortal.

Pat is buried in the midst of a Gullah community on Saint Helena Island, near his beloved town of Beaufort. The cemetery, Saint Helena Memorial Garden, is owned by Brick Baptist Church, which graciously allowed a non-Baptist, non–African American writer to rest among them. Pat chose that site because he was intrigued by the rich history of Brick Baptist Church, which was built by slaves in 1855, then turned over to them during Reconstruction; and by the church's connection to the nearby Penn Center, one of the first schools for freed slaves. Because Pat has written about his interest in Penn Center, the Memorial Garden is a fitting final resting place for him.

The graveyard is isolated, lovely and unpretentious, set amid a few lonesome pines and small live oaks. There are no grandiose tombstones nor lushly landscaped gardens, just proud, well-tended plots and loving mementos occasionally left among them: birthday cards, faded silk roses, deflated balloons, even a couple of fishing poles. The first time I visited Pat there, I wandered around rather aimlessly afterward, fighting off the overwhelming grief that threatened to do me in. I examined the nearby headstones halfheartedly, because my mind kept going back to a fresh mound of dirt surrounded by dying funeral wreaths. Soon, however, I got caught up in the very real human stories revealed on the stones: *Oh, look— some of them have photos by their names . . . What a great hat! . . . The lady over there was called Sweetie, and the one next to Pat was a seamstress.* When I saw that Arabelle Watson was buried there, on whom Pat based a character in *The Great Santini*, I hurried back over to Pat's lonely mound of dirt to tell him.

There was no need, of course. What was I thinking? Hadn't I seen the man at book signings enough to know what I had known from the moment I got to the graveyard, so devastated I barely knew where I was? A few days earlier, Pat had arrived here in a big fancy vehicle and was ushered to a place surrounded by expensive wreaths, some bearing cards with famous names on them. A kilted bagpiper played as a crowd of mostly white folks gathered. The ceremony was different, short and sweet, and many in the crowd crossed themselves after the prayers by the elegantly robed priests. Some of Pat's new neighbors must have watched the whole thing curiously and maybe even a bit suspiciously, wondering who on earth had landed among them.

The mourners didn't linger, and soon it was quiet again. But not for long. Before any of the occupants of the Memorial Garden knew what was happening, here comes this big beaming Irishman, with a mess of white hair, twinkling eyes, and an impish smile on his face. He strides among them, larger than life, and calls out, "Hey, folks, I'm Pat Conroy. Now tell me who you are. Isn't that Mr. Bradley? How many fish you caught today, sir? I promise not to put it in a book. Or if I do, I'll change your name, and double the number of fish. Arabelle, get yourself over here and give me a big hug! And tell me where Miss Smalls got that great hat. Bet it's got a story behind it. You know what? I'll bet that every single one of you has a story to tell me. C'mon now, don't be shy. No, wait—let me get a pen. I want to hear them all."

They look at each other, rolling their eyes, and some of them cover their mouths and laugh behind his back. But when he comes back with pen and paper, dusting the dirt off his navy blue jacket, they can't seem to help themselves. One by one, they begin to tell their stories, encouraged to go on by the gleam of excitement in his bright eyes. They talk and he writes down what they tell him, because they cannot stop themselves from doing so. Embellishing and expanding their words—their beautiful words!—he makes them come to life again, and through their stories, they live on. And as long as there are people like him to "open the light," to share the stories with the rest of us, they always will.

—*Cassandra King*

HEY,
OUT
THERE

||||||||||||||

The First Letter

||||||||||||

An Opening to the Light

AUGUST 3, 2009

Hello, out there,

This is the first letter I've ever written for a website, modern times seem to require it of all human beings. This website was produced by Mihai (Michael) Radulescu, my agent Marly Rusoff's partner, who spent a couple of hours explaining its intricacies and its cunning store of useless data concerning my own squirrelly life. I'm the only writer I know whose website bears the artistic mark of a native-born Romanian. The Internet remains a mystery to me as vast and untouchable as any ocean. I don't understand it but the wizards and snake handlers who control me tell me that all this is part of the inexplicable strangeness of the world we now inhabit.

My health went south on me this spring. In the middle of May, I began internally bleeding. I took this as a very bad sign that did not bode well for a frisky old age. My wife, Cassandra, drove me to the emergency room in Beaufort where my doctor, Lucius Laffitte, met me and got me to the Medical University of South Carolina. All the nurses and doctors there were spectacular. They saved my life.

Everything that was wrong with me that night was my fault. I had tantalized the Fates by embracing that life-defying trifecta: overeating, overdrinking, and lack of exercise. I'm trying to develop the appetite of a parakeet, drink nothing stronger than Clamato juice, and try to do aerobics in a Fripp Island pool as often as I can. When I enter the pool I look as though I'm trying out for a part as Moby-Dick. It's not a pretty sight.

The tour for *South of Broad* began at my house at Fripp this past week. The tour is abbreviated because of my health, which I regret. I always liked meeting and talking to you guys on the road, but that was at a time before airline travel became an American nightmare. I'll go by car on most of the signings, and we'll see how it goes. I'm alone in a room for most of my life, writing, and I love it when readers bring me news of the outside world. That part of my life might be coming to an end, and nothing fills me with more regret. To have attracted readers is the most magical part of my writing life. I was not expecting you to show up when I wrote my first books. It took me by surprise. It filled me with gratitude. It still does.

Yesterday, August 2, I took my agents to Charleston for a tour of the city. A young publicist from Random House, Elizabeth Johnson, went with us. She married a Marine Corps fighter pilot and they are stationed at the Marine Corps Air Station, where he is in training before shipping out to one of the war zones. I've always taken a childish joy in showing off Charleston to strangers in the city. Charleston never lets me down, but this time my tour of the city had an unusual twist. I showed them Charleston through the eyes of the narrator of *South of Broad*, Leo King. I followed Leo's paper route through the old part of the city, showed them the high points and low points of Leo's career as a child. I showed them the distinguished line of mansions that grace the jacket of the book. To me it composes the prettiest formation of houses in the book. We toured The Citadel and I pointed out the places I had lived when I was pretending to be a cadet. I owe The Citadel more than I can express in words. That day, The Citadel was beautiful in sunlight, and Charleston strutted in the beauty of all its strange elixirs. For lunch we ate at Magnolias; all four of us ordered seafood over grits: lobster, shrimp, and scallops with a lobster sauce. It was as good as food can get. Later I returned home. I remembered dozens of things I forgot to tell them. My new book has changed the way I see and present Charleston, and nothing makes me happier.

There are at least three books I want to write before I buy the farm, and I've already begun the first of those. In it, I'm visiting my real family for one final look, one last summation of all I learned from being part of that hurt and glorious tribe. I've written the first three chapters, and I'll try to finish it next year.

For the second book, Nan Talese wants me to write an Atlanta novel and I told her I would do it. Because of my illness I feel a great imperative to write faster and become more prolific as I limp toward my final chapter. And the third book is a novel about the first two years of teaching at Beaufort High School, when I fell in love with all the kids I taught. My friend Bernie Schein calls them "the best years" and I look back on them as the happiest of my life. I adored those students and they seemed to like me right back.

I close the first letter with relief and some anxiety. They tell me I should do this every now and then. In some ways it seems like a nightmare for someone who never learned to type, in other ways an opening to the light.

Great love out there . . .

Surprises on the Road

|||||||||||||

Hey, out there,
I returned to Fripp Island last Saturday after a driving tour around the South. It was tiring but exhilarating, and I rediscovered that I love meeting the people who read my books. They tell me stories. Some of them resurrect a past I had forgotten long ago. Citadel alumni turn out in large numbers. They tap Citadel rings with me before they leave the signing table. A grandmother who read *The Water Is Wide* the first year she taught English had me sign a book for her granddaughter, who had just begun her

first year as an English teacher. I listened to stories of the Iraq and Afghan wars.

Because of my cookbook, people brought me pound cakes, pickled shrimp, a dozen oysters, grits, boiled peanuts, heirloom tomatoes, crawdads, and other good things to eat. In Birmingham, I spoke to a crowd after the writer Rick Bragg and my comely wife, Cassandra King, warmed the audience up. It annoyed me that both Rick and Cassandra were funnier than I was and I could not help but notice the letdown and sense of disappointment that rushed through the crowd when I got up to speak. We then had dinner at Frank Stitt's magnificent restaurant, the Highlands Bar and Grill. Because I once wrote an introduction to one of his superb cookbooks, Frank and his staff feed me like a king whenever I am lucky enough to be in Birmingham.

In Charleston, I spoke briefly to the assembled groups and spotted Mike Mahoney, my longest-running friend in the world, grinning at me. I've known Mike since sixth grade, when my family moved to Culpeper Street in Arlington, Virginia. He was a great kid and proved to be a lifelong friend. His mother and two sisters were knockouts, and Mike and

I were altar boys when his mom, Kitty, married the irrepressible Don Mancini. Kitty has always served as a north star in my conflicted life. The Mahoney family took me in when I was a sixth-grader and have never let me go. Mike and his wife, Rita, recently retired and moved near coastal North Carolina. I promised to visit them soon.

My Citadel roommate, Mike De Vito, was there, and so was Dave Bornhorst, the heart and soul of my Citadel basketball team. I think I knew more than two hundred people in line and I had once asked one of them to marry me. I had met Marnie Huger when we applied for a job working with migrant workers and sat beside each other as we awaited our turn to be interviewed. She was as lovely a young woman as I had ever seen, and we dated that whole summer. Her family lived on Sullivan's Island and I was smitten with all of them. Marnie and I went out ten or twelve times that summer and I was happy just to be along for the ride. I wanted to marry the whole family. I began teaching at Beaufort High School in 1967. I wrote a letter to Marnie in college, and I have a distinct impression that I asked her to think about marrying me. As I look back on the callow boy I was, the letter must have struck Marnie as hilarious. She wrote me a sweet letter back, telling me how much the summer had meant to her and her family. Though flattered by my offer, she suggested that I think about holding her hand or kissing her if I were serious about approaching the altar with her. At the signing, Marnie gave me a long letter that she had written me. The letter was lovely, and I shall treasure it the rest of my life.

Being inside a bookstore stimulates my desire to read, and being on tour gives me lots of time to do so. Steve Rubin sent me a copy of John Grisham's book of short stories, *Ford County*, and I read it with pleasure and growing excitement. The short story seems like a majestic but difficult form to me and I had not known that John would prove so gifted in the art of the short story. I've known John for a while now and have read his books since he first catapulted onto the national stage with *The Firm*. He calls me periodically to chastise me for my occupational laziness and my shameless inability to produce a novel in this century. John works as hard as any novelist I've ever met, and I've been hooked on his books since he first started publishing with Doubleday. After admiring his short stories, I'm going to try to get him to write a book of poetry. I think he could pull it off.

Two other big boppers, John Irving and Richard Russo, have published books this season and they both burn brightly in the pantheon of writers I revere. Both these guys can't write a grocery list without it sounding like literature. I collect the work of both men and their books have proven to me that New England is every bit as quirky, eccentric, and character-rich as the South. Margaret Atwood's new book arrived at the house yesterday.

Last night, I finished a book, *Why This World: A Biography of Clarice Lispector*, by Benjamin Moser. Always, I hunt for great writers I've never heard of, and Clarice Lispector is considered to be one of the greatest female novelists in the history of Brazilian literature. In 1978 I got myself exposed to Latin American literature and I think it changed my life. I went through a long fruitful period when I read almost nothing else as I devoured the work of Márquez, Vargas Llosa, Borges, Carpentier, and a dozen others. If there is a better novel than *A Hundred Years of Solitude*, I don't know what it is. The oddly named Clarice Lispector had avoided my detection, yet I found the story of her life both improbable and riveting. I have ordered her novels and I await their arrival.

At my writing desk, I'm reading Robert Pinsky's

new anthology of poems, *Essential Pleasures*. I've always liked Pinsky's poetry and it's nice to see such refined taste in his choice of other poets.

There is another book out there that I need to talk about. My daughter, Melissa Conroy, has written and illustrated her first children's book. It is called *Poppy's Pants*. The great secret of the book is I am Poppy. My first grandchild, Elise Conroy, started calling me Poppy as soon as she began to talk. There was never any indication given about where this nickname came from, but the rest of the grandchildren have picked it up. Several years ago, Melissa took a drawing of me by her daughter Lila and made a doll, a Poppy doll, for her child. The doll looks like a whacked-out sumo wrestler on steroids, but Lila carried it around with her. I told my daughter that if I thought I really looked like that doll, I'd put my head into an oven. But my other grandchildren clamored for ones of their own and a cottage industry was begun. Blue Apple Books saw the dolls at an art show in New York and asked Melissa if she'd like to do a children's book. Melissa took a story from her own childhood and turned it into her first book.

Though I never noticed that I only wore khaki pants, my children certainly did. When Woo (my nickname for Melissa) was about five, she told me I had a hole in my khakis. She offered to sew them up for me and I accepted. When she asked me about what color she should use, I answered that I was color-blind and that I saw the world like a cocker spaniel saw it, not like a human being. Woo sewed it up using aquamarine thread because she wanted to add color to my monochromatic life. The result delighted me, and my daughters claim I wore the same khakis for at least three more years. I wrote an afterword to *Poppy's Pants* and am going to sign books with Melissa in the near future. She suggested I wear khaki pants. I suggested she sew them up with aquamarine thread.

Next in line is a nonfiction book called *My Reading Life*, about some of the books and people that have inspired me. It has been a joy to write.

I've already begun work on a new nonfiction book about my family with a great emphasis on my father's post-*Santini* life. My father managed to change his entire life after I wrote a novel about his brutal regime as a family man. It took resoluteness and courage for my father to change, and I need to acknowledge that. My brothers and sisters have all gotten nosebleeds and migraines since they heard news of this project.

I hope to write it in a year, while taking notes on my Atlanta novel.

A woman in Charlotte approached me and said that she's tired of the dysfunction in my novels. I told her I was sorry, but that is how the world has presented itself to me throughout my life. She told me her family was normal and they were proud of being a happy family with no clouds on the horizon. I congratulated her and told her I wished I had been raised in such a family.

Thank you for reading *South of Broad.* It is, as all of my novels have been, a love letter to all of you who read my books.

Great love out there . . .

The Fire Sermon

||||||||||||||

SPEECH BY PAT CONROY,

DELIVERED AT PENN CENTER

2010

Fifty years ago this October, Gene Norris brought me to Penn Center as a fifteen-year-old boy. The event was a community sing, and the first of the great spirituals I heard sung there was "The Old Sheep Done Know the Road." Ever since that night I've always thought that black people could sing a lot better than white people. Mr. Norris took me to the events at Penn Center for the rest of my high school and college life. It was at Penn that I met Dr. Martin Luther King on a street now named for him. I also met Ralph Abernathy, Andy Young, Jesse Jackson, Julian Bond, and the entire leadership of that fabulous civil rights movement that brought the South kicking and screaming into the twentieth century. I felt a part of it because I observed some of its evolvement at Penn Center, a witness to its very creation. I watched my whole country change because of meetings that had taken place at Penn Center. I fell in love with the sons and daughters of slaves that lived on Saint Helena Island, and Mr. Norris told me I was walking amidst the first men and women ever emancipated from slavery in the American South.

Few people understood the exceptional role the civil rights movement had on the white boys and girls of the South. Bill Clinton would never have become who he was without the shining example of Martin Luther King. The same is true of Jimmy Carter and Fritz Hollings and Richard and Joe Riley. Imagine this: you're a little white kid and you watch fire hoses turned on people who don't seem to be hurting anyone, and fierce dogs being turned on young men who carry signs about freedom. We white kids grew up watching movies and TV and guess what we had learned to do? We had learned to tell the good guys from the bad guys. One night I found my mother weeping while watching the evening news. She was watching a news clip of the Montgomery Bus Boycott, where thousands of black men and women were walking to work on the streets of that old Confederate capital. My mother was touched by the unearthly dignity of a people on the march who were fighting by refusing to fight—whose immense strength lay in their allegiance to nonviolence.

In 1962, one hundred years after the founding of Penn School, Peggy Conroy, with the help of Gene Norris, integrated the Marine Corps Officers' Club in Beaufort. She had come to a community sing at Penn after hearing my rave reviews of those stirring performances. She was the president of the Officers' Wives' Club and invited the choir at Robert Smalls High School over to sing spirituals. The choir knocked the socks off those pretty Marine wives, and desegregation took another small step in the South.

When I was a sophomore at The Citadel, I received a phone call from Gene Norris asking me to infiltrate a meeting of the Ku Klux Klan. He had me call Sheriff Wallace, who told me he had received reports that the Klan was planning to incite the mob to storm out of Saint Helena's and burn down the home of Courtney and Elizabeth Siceloff at Penn Center. Sheriff Wallace wanted me to attend the rally and call from a phone booth at a nearby cheesy motel.

"Can you pretend to be a redneck, Pat?" he asked.

"I went to Beaufort High. I'm an expert at playing redneck."

So, I attended my first Klan meeting and milled among the white-robed figures, surprised when people started calling out my name. I met six or seven young men I had played against in football, basketball, or baseball—guys from Hampton, Edisto, Orangeburg, and Ridgeland. One guy expressed surprise at my interest in the Klan and asked me, "Pat, aren't you a Roman Catholic?"

"C'mon, Bubba. Where on earth did you get that idea? I've been Southern Baptist since birth," I lied, denying the faith of my fathers.

After they burned the cross, I went to the telephone booth and called Sheriff Wallace to tell him that neither Penn Center nor the Siceloffs were mentioned, and everyone seemed to be going home.

"What was the meeting for?"

Sheriff Wallace laughed when I said, "The Klan doesn't seem to like black people very much."

So I came to Penn Center fifty years ago, and Penn Center does me high honor tonight. Penn Center led me by the hand to a destiny that made me a teacher, that made me become a teacher of Afro-American history, the first such course taught in a formerly white high school in South Carolina. When a job opened up on an isolated Daufuskie Island, I asked for the job because I wanted to be part of history. I knew I'd be the first white man ever to teach black children in that portion of the world and I thought I'd be doing God's work. I did God's work with eighteen of his sweetest children.

An official from the school district visited my school at Daufuskie after I'd been there for a month. After strolling through my class, this man commented, "Too bad they're all retards."

"Come back in a month. I'll have a surprise for you. And don't ever call my kids that again."

He returned with four people from the county office the next month. Me and my kids were ready and waiting. My mother had given me one of her cheapo birthday presents that had the fifty greatest classical hits on it—everyone from Beethoven to Handel. Each day, I'd play that record at the end of school.

"Okay, kids, this is Beethoven's Fifth Symphony. Raise your hands when you hear death knocking at the door. Fall asleep when you hear Brahms's lullaby.

Run for your life, Rimsky-Korsakov's *Flight of the Bumblebee*'s on the way."

When those school officials walked into that room, a woman supervisor said that the music I was playing was inappropriate for children this young.

"Sallie Ann," I said to my introductress in the sixth grade, "this nice lady thinks that music is inappropriate."

"Perhaps she'd rather listen to Rimsky-Korsakov," Sallie Ann said. "Or perhaps Tchaikovsky."

I went straight through the fifty top classical hits and my kids nailed every one of them. The five officials left stunned, and were angry when I offered to test them in front of the kids.

"Most inappropriate," the same woman said.

"That's because none of you know the music."

Last night, my old friend John Gadsen remembered the days of my youth when I was a hothead. I do not think I was a hothead—not then and not now. I thought I was right. I had read the Declaration of Independence, the Constitution, and the Bible. Segregation seemed evil from the time I was a boy. Slavery is an abomination on the American soul, an ineradicable stain on our body politic. But Penn Center lit a fire that has never gone out, and the election of President Barack Obama was one of the happiest days of my life.

You know how my story as a teacher ended. The white boys rose up and got rid of this hotheaded white boy. I never taught again. The white boys won, or so they thought. That superintendent and that school board drove me out of a job and eventually out of Beaufort. But to you, the people of Penn Center, whose ancestors survived the grueling Middle Passage and the heat of cotton fields and the whips of overseers—rejoice with me. I'm living proof that Penn Center can change a white boy's life. You changed me utterly and I'm forever grateful to you. Yes, I was fired, humiliated, and run out of town because I believed what Martin Luther King believed. Yes, they got me good, Penn Center, but on this joyous night, let me brag to you at last: Didn't I get those sorry sons of bitches back?

Thank you very much . . .

On the Future of Books

||||||||||||

H ey, out there,
 About the war between me and technology: it appears that technology is rolling over
me like a blitzkrieg. I'm a victim of all its barbarisms.
I still can't type, which makes my e-mails seem composed by a highlands baboon. Once or twice a week,
I check my e-mail, whether I need to or not. I understand that most human beings check theirs with more
frequency. Twitter is an unknown factor in my life
and I've never seen Facebook, even though I'm told I
have a presence on both of these entities. People give
me looks of pity and ask me why I want to wallow

in my disconnection from a very connected world. It is simple. The world seems way too connected to me now. It seems to be ruining the lives of teenagers and bringing out the bestial cruelty in those who can hide their vileness under the mask of some idiotic pseudonym. I like to sit alone and think about things. Solitude is as precious as coin silver and it takes labor to attain it. I can be frivolous without Twitter and Facebook. I turned sixty-five this year and I take old age seriously. There's work to be done.

Oh, by the way, I don't own a Kindle or an iPad or one of those fancy cell phones where I can type up a novel or read *The New York Times* or build a boat in my living room. My younger friends tell me that Kindle is an absolutely revolutionary invention, and I'll admit that the thought of downloading *Anna Karenina* and reading it on a cross-country flight is astonishing to me. Even so, I'll remain a book guy because I own eight thousand of them and I love the way they make my house look. The publishing world seems to have been caught flat-footed by the sheer brilliance of this assault, and we've come to a point where the future of books is at stake. What remains certain is that any writer in the world can now get a book published without the help of agents, editors, or even a publishing house. I encourage every unpublished writer to do just that. Then, I would get fifteen real books in hardback from Books on Demand to give myself, friends, and family. My first book, *The Boo*, was published by McClure Press in Virginia, and my mother gave me a launch party at her house on East Street in Beaufort. I remember The Boo himself giving me the presentation copy of the book and signing it. Just now, I looked at what he signed and it moved me greatly. "To the lamb that made me. The Boo." I know much about the pleasures of publishing your own book.

Great love . . .

My Spooky Life

||||||||||||||

Hey, out there,
   When I used to keep journals on a fairly regular basis, I thought I was reporting on my own spooky, invisible interior life. This letter—or blog—has the same feel to it, and I find it a great warm-up for a day at the writing table. After a month of traveling and running my mouth (is there anyone on earth sicker of the sound of his own voice than me?), I've returned to work on the book called *The Death of Santini*. I've written more about my parents than any writer in the history of the world, and I still

return to their mysterious effigies as I try to figure out what it all means—some kind of annunciation or maybe even a summing-up. They still exert immense control over me even though they've been dead for so long. But I can conjure up their images without exerting a thimbleful of effort. Both of them act like lawyers on call, and they seem to take pleasure in their daily visits to plead their cases before their seven children.

I was on the phone with my brother Jim the other night when he tossed me this little circle of gold from our past. Jim is a hotshot salesman who works for Ruiz Foods, based in Dinuba, California. He is called the "dark one" in the family, and it is a sobriquet well earned, although there are mother lodes of darkness in each one of us. Jim told me about the last time he visited our grandmother Stanny in her last years in assisted living in Orlando. Jim's work brought him to the area every six months. Toward the end, Stanny got dementia and she never recognized Jim when he came to see her. The last time he saw her, Jim entered Stanny's room and gave her a kiss on the cheek as she sat in her wheelchair.

"Hello, young man," she said. "I don't believe I know you, do I?"

"Yes, you do, Stanny," Jim replied.

"Could you explain how?"

"I'd be happy to, Stanny. I'm your grandson Jim. I'm the fifth child of your daughter, Peg Conroy. My father is Don Conroy."

"Oh, no. That couldn't be true," Stanny said.

"It's true," Jim told her. "I'm the fifth child of Peg and Don Conroy. Remember, Pat's the oldest? Then there is Carol, Mike, and Kathy. I came right after them. Tim and Tom were your last grandchildren born in that family."

"No, that just can't be true," Stanny argued.

"Why not?" Jim asked, puzzled.

"Because my daughter Peggy was a very beautiful woman. Her husband, Don, was a very handsome man."

"That's true, but I still don't get it."

Stanny looked hard at Jim and said, "You are a very ugly young man. You could not possibly be their son."

As Jim told the story I waited for the "dark one" to emerge. He did when he told our grandmother, "Hey, Stanny. Have you looked in the mirror lately?"

Jim reported that both he and Stanny laughed so

hard that he thought they would cry. Humor has always been the redemptive angel in the Conroys' sad history. With this family, I shall never grow hungry from lack of material.

Great love . . .

My Blogging Life

||||||||||||||

AUGUST 2, 2011

Hey, out there,
I've published two books since I first wrote a letter of introduction to my newly hatched website. For me, this is a starting-out point caused mostly by the passage of time and the possibility of my sudden or protracted death. Now, I'm halfway through a new book I'm calling *The Death of Santini*, in which I tell of my father's miraculous turnaround after he retired from the Marine Corps. He loathed my depiction of him in *The Great Santini*, and he set out to prove me wrong by turning himself into something that was recognizably human. It's the

great surprise of my life that I ended up loving him so much. My brothers and sister Kathy are unloading their stories about Mom and Dad to me, and we all suffered in the house of Santini. My siblings do not all share my exalted affection for our mother, and I have not been shy about sharing their dissent. This causes me pain, but I've been writing about these two mismatched people for my whole life, so I need to get to some kind of conclusion about them, one that feels like the truth at last.

My sister Carol Ann remains a stranger to my life. I only see her at weddings and funerals—all of which she turns into personal nightmares for me— as you will one day read about. My sisters-in-law are so hysterical at the thought of reading about themselves and their poor, traumatized husbands that they have been treating me with far more kindness and respect than they could ever muster in the past. I tell them that they have nothing to worry about, but they know that I've lied before. (That's a joke, girls.)

In the late nineties I was diagnosed with an incurable neurological disorder known as "writer's cramp." Though I laughed out loud when the doctor gave me this diagnosis, the humor of it faded in short order. It's the same disease that Henry James developed, and it sent him to a recording device to speak his novels into a machine and have them transcribed. In my opinion this did not help the later novels much, and I can't pick up *The Golden Bowl* or *The Princess Casamassima* without choking on the runaway elaborations of his spoken novelistic voice.

So I did not buy a tape recorder or invest in a computer that operates by voice recognition, as the supremely gifted writer Richard Powers did. Instead, I did wrist exercises and managed to write on my "good days," read on the bad ones. The main thing that changed was that I rarely wrote in my journals at all. I could not afford to sacrifice my writing life to the luxury of journal keeping when there were more novels to write. I checked out the blog world, "blog" being the ugliest word to emerge out of the "wired" universe so far. But, I thought, I've got this website that I barely use, and it's being watched over by a baleful webmaster, Mihai (Michael) Radulescu, who hails from Romania where Vlad the Impaler and Count Dracula once left their marks. I'll make an effort to keep this journal until I decide to abandon it and return happily to my unjournaled life.

Great love . . .

The Boo's Lambs Gather
in Charleston

||||||||||||

Hey, out there,
   My classmates in Romeo Company at
The Citadel are beginning to stir and gather.
As the country paused to remember the firing on Fort
Sumter, it made me remember that I went to the col-
lege whose cadets fired the first shots in the Civil War
and that two of my classmates in R Company were
named for Southern generals—Stonewall Jackson
Watson and Wade Hampton Williford III.

   I spoke at the Citadel library last month, at an
event honoring the publication of my friend John
Warley's new novel called *Bethesda's Child*. John and

I roomed together on the Citadel baseball team and have been lifelong friends ever since those faraway days. I wrote a thirteen-page introduction to his book, and it reminded me of our times on that wonderful team with road trips through the South which still remain legendary to me and John. He and I are going to be doing a talk together next year at the Savannah Book Festival. John and his wife, Barbara, are our neighbors now that Cassandra and I have moved into Beaufort. We have lunch on a weekly basis to reminisce about our time at The Citadel together.

After the talk at The Citadel, John and I went out to a restaurant bar on Queen Street with three of my classmates from Romeo Company. Unfortunately, John Warley was a slovenly, uncouth member of Tango Company, the tallest company at the college, but also the dumbest and least military. My R Company guys griped all evening that I had loused up the experience by bringing along a "waste from Tango," but John is silver-tongued and quick, and he more than held his own. The horror of all Citadel wives is to put up with their husbands and their classmates telling Citadel stories that they've heard a thousand times before. I admit, there is some repetition at play.

I'd never met Robbie Schear's wife before, though I knew of her when they dated at The Citadel. Nancy Miller was selected "Miss Citadel" for our senior year and remains a stunning woman today. Stonewall Jackson Watson brought his delightful daughter, Meg, who has a lot better personality than her father ever did.

We talked of many things that night, ranging from Hell Night to members of the R Company cache we still hated with all the powers of abhorrence we could summon. But someone mentioned The Boo and I realized I had never stopped grieving over The Boo's death. For those readers who don't know, The Boo was Lieutenant Colonel Thomas Nugent Courvoisie, the assistant commandant of cadets at The Citadel and the subject of my first book, *The Boo*. I often tell people *The Boo* is "the worst book ever written by an American," and I wish I'd written it better. But the evening made me think a lot about The Boo, who is buried near my parents in the Beaufort National Cemetery. I was scared of him at The Citadel, but he was a source of humanity and justice, and the most beloved man on campus during his brief time among the cadets. I went looking for the presentation copy of

The Boo he had given me in 1970. I had never opened it that I could remember, and I wanted to see if he had signed it. When I opened it, I found these eight words written to me forty-one years ago: "To the lamb who made me, The Boo." These words made my whole writing career worthwhile.

And I have begun thinking of that life as miraculous and lucky. How could a man I had dreaded as my commandant and who tried twice to get me kicked out of college become the subject of the first book I would write? How could the young kid I was then become one of the closest friends The Boo would ever make? Who could have predicted that The Boo would be hired as the mighty advisor for the filming of *The Lords of Discipline* in England? After his long humiliation and exile by The Citadel, who would have predicted that he and I would both be honored by a full-dress parade and honorary degrees as we stood shoulder-to-shoulder on the same parade ground we had marched on as boys? Who could have foreseen the day I would deliver his eulogy at the Summerall Chapel, or that I would give a speech on the night they named the dining room in the new Alumni Hall after him? Not me. Not once. Not ever.

I thought you might like to read the speech I gave when they dedicated "The Boo's room." It was a great night, and The Boo's lambs have always been rowdy, loud, and attracted to the wild side.

There is one great story about The Boo that has never been told, and I waited for a night like this to tell it. In 1969, The Boo was removed from his position as the assistant commandant of cadets in charge of discipline and sent in exile to The Citadel warehouse, where he spent the rest of his career in charge of cadet luggage and supplying the entire campus with custodial material and toilet paper. He was given a direct order that he was to have nothing to do with Citadel cadets except those who had business at the warehouse. Always the good soldier, The Boo did as he was told and his personal contact with cadets before he retired in 1982 was minimal. In those years, The Citadel learned it could hide the growing legend of The Boo, but could not bury it. The Citadel found out that it could not hide what the Corps revered; it could not sweep under the rug what the Corps deeply loved. The Boo had proven he could love a whole Corps of Cadets like no man who ever put on a Citadel ring. It came time for the Corps to pay him back.

In 1973, The Boo had a heart attack that almost killed him. I drove down from Atlanta to visit him at the naval hospital, and he did not look that day like a man who would survive to see the dedication of the Courvoisie Room in September of 2001. When I left to return to Atlanta the next day, Elizabeth Courvoisie wept at my departure and told me she did not ever think I would see her husband again. Two weeks later, he returned to his quarters in the Citadel campus, bedridden and despondent. For a month, he did not leave his house. Only a few cadets came to visit him because The Boo had become invisible to the Corps of Cadets, or so The Citadel thought. So The Boo thought.

Nothing on earth thinks or moves or acts or responds like The Citadel Corps of Cadets. The Corps of Cadets is a sovereign nation unto itself, a country that fashions its own rules, a strange entity that makes up its own mind in its own good time. The Citadel thought the Corps of Cadets had forgotten the legend of The Boo. But it was the Corps who made that legend and the Corps who would keep it alive.

Word spread that The Boo was critically ill. A rumor had it that he was dying. Along the galleries, cadets gathered to talk, and the rumors began to fly, and nowhere does rumor travel faster than the Corps. Because they are cadets, there is always mischief and always daring, always a sense of humor that is deeper than anything else. A plan was hatched in secret.

At parade the following Friday, the Board of Visitors and General Duckett stood and saluted as the Corps passed in review before them, as they had done on a thousand Fridays before. But this time, parade was destined to be unlike any Citadel parade before or since in the many-storied and many-splendored history of our college. This parade belongs to the ages. When the A Company commander marched his troops off the field, his company was nearing the street in front of Third Battalion where he would issue the traditional order of "Company right, march." In the first time since The Citadel moved to its new home by the Ashley River, the A Company commander

ordered his three platoons to march to the left.
He was followed by the commander of Bravo
company, of Charlie, of Delta, of Echo, and
then by every company in the Corps. On the
street between the Third and Fourth Battalions,
Alpha Company marched right toward the mess
hall and the infirmary, with the entire Corps
of Cadets behind them. At the infirmary, the
Corps turned left again and only two people on
the campus knew what the Corps of Cadets was
up to.

The Boo had spent the day shining up. "The
cadets won't care if you're shined up or not,"
Elizabeth Courvoisie said to her husband.

"I expect the Corps to be sharp for me," The
Boo said. "I want to be sharp for them."

When the boys of Alpha reached his house,
and the A Company commander gave the
command of "Eyes right," the guidon snapped
in the cool autumn air. The Boo, in uniform,
returned the salute with perfect military bearing
and held it until A Company had passed. Then
he saluted Bravo and Charlie, on down to
Romeo and Tango and the Band.

The man who had not been out of his

home for ninety days, and the man who had
not returned to work for a single day, held his
salute as seventeen companies passed in view
for a man that none of them knew. Here is
the significance of that thrilling, rogue parade,
which in the highly structured world of The
Citadel was a revolutionary act. The Corps of
Cadets broke ranks and all the rules of order
that applied to the Friday parade to pay homage
to the man who was in charge of cadet luggage.
The Corps has never broken ranks to honor
General Summerall or Mark Clark or Prince
Charles or Ronald Reagan or any member of
the Board of Visitors or the generals of any army
of the world. The Corps did it once and only
once, and they did it for the love of The Boo, a
man they knew only by the power of his legend,
by the greatness of his story. And nothing moves
the Corps like the power of love.

That power has gathered us together tonight.
It is here that we will pass in review for The Boo
one last time. We will name this room for him
and him alone. Lieutenant Colonel Thomas
Nugent Courvoisie has now written his name
into the stones of our college, long after he wrote

his name in our memories and hearts. Once
The Boo roamed this campus fierce, alert, and
lion-voiced, and his wrath was a terrible thing.
He could scream and rant and call us "bums" a
thousand times, but he could not hide his clear
and overwhelming love of the Corps. The Corps
received that love, took it in, felt it in the deepest
places, and now, tonight, we give it back at the
school where we started out and we give it to
The Boo, as a gift, because once, many years ago,
The Boo loved us first, when we were cadets of
boys and when we needed it the most.

Boo, your bums salute you, sir, and we give
you this room, and we do it for love of you and
the ring.

Great love . . .

Hitch-22

||||||||||||

A GREAT MEMOIR

DECEMBER 17, 2011

Hey, out there,

Last night, I finished a splendid memoir written by the irascible and charming Christopher Hitchens. It is called *Hitch-22*, and the title reminded me of the time I found myself talking to a fascinating man at the deep end of a swimming pool in New Orleans. He turned out to be Joseph Heller. I always get a cheap literary thrill whenever I have these chance encounters on the road. I first started admiring Mr. Hitchens when he began writing his bristling, fire-eating essays in *Vanity Fair*. Over the years he began displaying that rarest of intellectual gifts—the ability and willingness to change his mind and do it in an orderly, well-reasoned way. He writes with a prose style that has teeth and venom and beauty. Hitchens is one of those uncommon writers who seem incapable of writing a boring sentence or thinking a banal thought.

There are surprises galore in this feast of a book, which is an intellectual treasure-house and a reader's delight. He is tenderhearted and clear-eyed in his portraits of his family and friends. I have always been attracted to male writers who can demonstrate their love and affection for women with ease, yet not draw attention to themselves. In a chapter of admirable clarity, he finally reveals what goes on in those infamous British public schools that have tortured every male writer who ever wrote a novel or memoir about the English path to enlightenment. He clears up the mysteries of that charged, homoerotic environment and does it in a way that is explanatory and not a bit sensational or exploitative.

Mr. Hitchens writes about the importance of friendships as well as any writer I've ever read. In his chapter on his long friendship with Martin Amis, he creates a masterly portrait that made me want to be friends with both men and regret that I had once had that possibility in my life, but had failed to make the right move in that direction. Once, a lifetime away, I had been part of the creation of a movie development company, and the first book we bought for our first film was *The Rachel Papers* by Martin Amis. I had read the book in galleys and knew a hotshot when I saw one. Mr. Amis was a young gun fresh out of the box and he wrote with verve, precision, and cunning. I could have met him, and *Hitch-22* made me think not doing so was one of the great errors of my life. The choices I didn't make are almost as ruinous as the ones I did.

Mr. Hitchens's portraits of Salman Rushdie, James Fenton, Edward Said, and Susan Sontag are all superb and enlightening. His intellectual life and his curiosity are insatiable. As a political figure, he reminds me of the great George Orwell, and he sprinkles accolades to Orwell all throughout the book. He takes you on journeys to Sarajevo, Kurdish territory in northern Iraq, uprisings and wars in sorrowful countries around the world. Often he places himself in grave danger and he never equivocates about whose side he's on. I didn't agree with President Bush's invasion of Iraq, but Mr. Hitchens makes the best case for that war I ever encountered. His portrait of Saddam Hussein is nothing short of satanic. If you can read what Hitchens has to say about Hussein and not at least reconsider your views on Iraq, I question your capacity to read.

He is the happiest of atheists and a heretic of charming godliness. I know Southerners who have Hitch on their prayer chains after hearing about (not reading) his homage to atheism, *God Is Not Great*. For some reason, I think these prayer chains will never succeed in leading Hitch to the steps of the Church of God. He sees that the intellectual life of the mind is the only sensible place on earth to be. When the idiot pastor Terry Jones burned the Koran, and the resulting protests among the Muslims of Afghanistan resulted in eleven killed, Christopher Hitchens was certainly not ambushed by surprise. A hell of a book.

Great love . . .

The Night the Band Played the
"Tennessee Waltz"

||||||||||||||

JULY 21, 2012

Hey, out there,
 I was flipping through some old journals of mine. It has caused me much grief that I've never been completely seduced by the craft of journal keeping. A laziness of soul takes over, and I abandon most of them over the course of a summer. But I sometimes find that I've forgotten something that I've been lucky to forget.

On January 11, 2000, an event occurred in the Beaufort First Presbyterian Church that took me by surprise. Once a year, I accompany Mrs. Julia Randel to church, and she always gets the superb choir to sing

"Blessed Assurance," a hymn I fell in love with when her son, Derril, died at age thirty-four. Tragically, Mrs. Randel has lost two sons, Derril and Randy. She is my mother figure in Beaufort, bequeathed to me when her fifteen-year-old son died in front of me on a baseball field—a transfiguring scene in my boyhood.

After the services ended that day, a stranger tapped me on the shoulder and asked me how I knew Janet Tetu.

I turned around and said, "I had a crush on Janet Tetu when I was in eighth grade."

"She's my lawyer in Columbia, a great one."

I called Janet Tetu Butcher that night. *Janet Tetu.* They were, at one time, the most magical four syllables in language to me. I fell in love with Janet in the eighth-grade class terrorized by the fiercest nun of my childhood, the dreaded Sister Mary Petra. There was one sweet kid who sat directly in front of me, and he had an intestinal condition. This poor creature would send out thunderous farts a couple of times a day, which brought Petra's wrath out of its cave. She would clench her fist and knock—yes, I still remember his name—this poor boy out of his chair. During a test in November, this boy let out a fart that could be heard at the White House. Petra looked ready to kill as she jumped out of her chair and made her way to exterminate the gaseous one. To my utter shock, the kid turned and pointed to me, "It was Conroy, Sister. I swear it was Conroy."

Before I could utter a word in my own defense, Sister Petra had put me on the floor with a fierce right cross that made my ear numb for the rest of the day. Enraged by the injustice, I returned to my seat and my test, and prayed that the trembling kid in front of me would hold his fire for the rest of the afternoon. He turned around to deliver anguished apologies for his action when Petra left the room. I'd forgiven him long before the bell rang.

Later that year, the trollish nun spotted the pretty Janet Tetu passing a note in class. Petra acted like Janet had spit on the Christ child and made her kneel on her knees for an hour, praying for her immortal soul. As we talked on the phone, Janet talked about the traumatizing effect that this punishment had on her; she refused to apply to a Catholic high school after that painful humiliation in front of her peers. I told her I wished she'd passed a note every day during the school year because I had spent a pleasurable and voyeurish hour simply starring at her oval-faced beauty.

Janet admitted she did not remember me at all. Nor could she come up with a single name of her female classmates. The only name she could conjure up was that of the darkly handsome David Keaney, who remains for me to this day the exemplar by which I measure all male beauty. She also remembered liking a boy named Steve.

"That was Steve Lickweg," I said. "He was a great guy."

"How do you remember that?" Janet asked.

"I was lonelier than you?"

But Janet had given me some correlation of how I saw myself as a boy—that I was invisible to the world around me. I asked her if she remembered a boy named Paul Kennedy, and she did not. His parents gave him a graduation party at the Officers' Club at Fort Myers, and I was thrilled to be seated next to her.

"I don't remember this at all," she said. "Why were you thrilled?"

"Because I had a crush on you."

"I didn't know that."

"Of course you didn't," I told her. "I couldn't even speak to a girl at that time in my life."

"I didn't know that," Janet said. "Pat, I don't remember anything you are talking about."

"Of course you didn't, Janet. But I can give you a glimpse of yourself that you didn't know about. I was afraid you wouldn't talk to me that night. But you were perfectly lovely—charming and friendly and dazzling—everything I hoped you'd be and more. You wore a white dress. You seemed to like me. That meant everything to me. I've pressed the memory of that night to my heart a dozen times and it happened over forty years ago, Janet Tetu."

"You put my name in *Beach Music*. That's how I found you."

"I've tried to thank everyone who was nice to me in my childhood—the list is not large."

"There's something you don't know about me, Pat."

"What's that?"

"I stood in line to get *Beach Music* signed in Columbia."

"Why didn't you tell me who you were?" I asked.

"Because I didn't know who you were," Janet said. "I didn't know I had a part in your life. I was reading *Beach Music* while my husband was driving down to the beach when I came across my name; I let out a yell. 'Tetu'—it means headstrong in French."

"Margaret Evans worked for me as a research assistant for *Beach Music,*" I said. "She calls these things my little salutes. Your salute finally arrived, and this phone call is my payoff."

"There are other amazing things, Pat. My husband is a '63 Citadel grad named Jim Butcher. You signed his personal copy of *The Lords of Discipline.* My son is a Citadel grad, Class of '95. He became an English major at The Citadel because he loved your work."

"My mother knew all about you, Janet. She studied you on the playground when she took her turn monitoring at recess. She gave you a high approval rating and thought you had class. From then on, whenever I liked a new girl, my mom would say, 'She's nice, Pat, but she is no Janet Tetu.' Before you, it was a girl in my kindergarten, and my mom would say, 'She's nice, Pat. But she's no Muffett Adams.'"

"You ever find Muffett?" Janet asked.

"I signed a copy of *The Prince of Tides* for her in Atlanta. I told Muffett that because of her I know that a boy can fall in love with a girl at the age of five."

"I saw you give a speech at the Thomas Cooper Society and wrote you a long letter once."

"I'm sorry we didn't connect, Janet. I also associate you with olives."

"Olives?" she said.

"At that same graduation, I saw you take something from a small dish and put it in your mouth."

"You didn't know what an olive was?"

"No, and I had asparagus that night for the first time. Mom didn't run an adventurous kitchen. So I walked on the wild side and popped that olive in my mouth. I bit down hard on it and almost broke a tooth on the pit. The pit was a complete surprise. Because I was sitting by the woman I loved, I suffered a real dilemma. The olive pit felt as large as a golf ball in my mouth. I knew I could not just spit the mangled, saliva-stained mess onto my plate. Nor did I have a clue about the etiquette of removing such a thing from my mouth. So, speechless, I sat there contemplating my next move. Finally, I mumbled my excuses and made a dash to the men's room, where I spat the disfigured olive into my hand. I slid the meat of the olive from the pit and tasted it. That's the first night I knew I loved olives. When I returned I asked you to dance. You were the first girl I ever danced with. The band played the 'Tennessee Waltz,' one of my mom and dad's favorite songs. That was the night of the comely and adored Janet Tetu, when she walked out of my life in a white dress, and stepped very prettily into her own."

We'll be friends for the rest of our lives.

Great love . . .

The Man Who Inspired *My Losing Season*
Left Us Too Soon . . .

||||||||||||

Hey, out there,
My basketball teammate John DeBrosse died September 25, 2013, in Dayton, Ohio. He was the shooting guard on the Citadel team I wrote about in my book *My Losing Season*. It was John's surprising and unexpected arrival at a book signing for *Beach Music* that reignited a friendship I'd lost when I graduated. I spotted him wandering through the aisles of books, looking as awkward as a wildebeest in the shopping mall where I was signing.

"Hey, DeBrosse, you ever been in a bookstore before?" I asked.

"Once, Conroy," he came back fast, as he always had. "I was lost."

"You ever read any of my books, DeBrosse?" I said.

"I tried once. They all sucked. Just like their author," John said. "Hey, Conroy, would you come home and meet my wife and family? They think I make this shit up. They don't think I know you at all."

That ride into the Dayton night with John DeBrosse changed the course of my whole life and the arc of my career. We talked about the team we played on together in 1966–67—that humiliated, beaten-down tribe who staggered to an 8–17 record and felt lucky to win eight games. The painfulness of that year lay etched in DeBrosse's round Ohio face as he described his mortification over a losing season that'd happened thirty years ago.

When he began to discuss the last game we ever played together, he asked me if I remembered a layup that he had missed in the final minute of a tournament game against Richmond. I told him I remembered the moment down to its last painful detail.

"I didn't miss layups, Conroy," he said with sudden fierceness. "I never missed a layup in my life."

"It didn't come at a good time, John," I said, knowing that the missed layup had cost us the game and our chance to meet West Virginia in the semifinals of the Southern Conference tournament.

At the next red light, John DeBrosse reached across the van and squeezed my wrist hard. "I didn't miss that layup on purpose, Conroy. I promise I didn't miss on purpose."

I laughed and said, "Of course you didn't, John. You couldn't even think like that."

"Our coach did. Mel Thompson thought I missed that shot on purpose because I knew I could get him fired."

"Hell, I'd have missed the layup if I thought Mel would've gotten fired," I said.

My long conversations with DeBrosse that night led to the writing of *My Losing Season*. I tracked down all my teammates and my coach and interviewed them about every single aspect of that disheartening year. I listened to grown men cry about their frustrations and failures and resentments of that long-ago season. I ended up falling in love with their families and children and could feel that love returned in full measure. In the end, my team came together again because the book turned us into the team we should have been, but never could be. It might be the best book I ever will write. It all began when John DeBrosse walked into a bookstore for the first time in his life.

My shooting guard, John DeBrosse, died this past Wednesday after being in a coma for a week. I was in New Orleans when I talked to his wife, Pam, and she told me that their children had assembled in the room to discuss taking him off life support. I cried on the phone, but Pam was rocklike and spent her time comforting me. She and John used to come to Fripp Island to spend weeks in our summerhouse. Every time I'd see John, he'd bring up that godforsaken season again and again. It especially galled John that Coach Thompson had named me most valuable player on that undeserving team when John had enjoyed a far better season than I had. With humor and some petulance, John would grab my tarnished trophy and walk with it around the Fripp Island house.

"I'm taking it, Conroy. It's mine. I earned it and you didn't," DeBrosse would say.

"I'll let you sleep with it, DeBrosse," I said. "Or you could take it for rides in Beaufort. But bring it back, loser. It belongs to me."

"You, the most valuable player? The worst player on the team gets MVP. And you're a Bolshevik who voted for Obama," John would say, fuming. "How did you get to be a communist going to a school like The Citadel, Conroy?"

"I met so many nice Nazis like you, John," I'd say, taking the trophy back, "it was easy."

"That MVP award? That trophy should be in my house and not yours."

"You didn't deserve it. You missed that layup on purpose and got our poor coach fired," I said, as John grabbed the trophy again and held it in his lap.

In the time we were young men together, John and I were part of an American generation of males who had no clear ways to talk emotionally with each other. We had to invent a language that only we could understand and interpret. We would curse each other and knock each other all over the court and elbow our way to the basket and stick our forearms into the chests of those who came at us in the controlled fury of games. Even as adults, DeBrosse and I would pick at each other, mouthing off as we showed off to our wives and kids, and turning almost boylike again when surrounded by our own teammates from that lost, ugly year. But I knew the secrets of how men communicate by observing DeBrosse and my teammates as we gathered ourselves together after *My Losing Season* came out. When we cuss each other out, call each other the vilest names on earth, and put each other down with thoughtless cruelty, it is the only way we know and the only language we have to express our ardent love for each other. John and I were men of a lock-jawed generation who lacked a specific language to communicate in the deepest places those hardest of things.

Dave Bornhorst and Doug Bridges are going to the funeral to represent our team. I'm on a book tour and cannot, to my shame and guilt, attend. But Dave and Doug are carrying up a memento from those days of anguish and friendship. They are taking a huge basketball trophy up with them to present to the family with a plaque that reads:

JOHN DeBROSSE
MOST VALUABLE PLAYER
THE CITADEL BASKETBALL TEAM 1966–67
FROM HIS TEAMMATES IN *MY LOSING SEASON*

Before John died, I asked Pam to do something for me as a favor. I asked her to kiss John for me, then whisper these words into his ear:

"Hey, John DeBrosse, your point guard says good-bye and he'll love you the rest of his life. Thanks for giving me *My Losing Season.*"

Pam did so.

Great love . . .

A Room of Her Own . . . and the
Birth of *Moonrise*

||||||||||||||

Hey, out there,

To write about your own wife's novel should cause shame to any serious writer, but in this case I find that I can do it with pleasure and a strong sense of pride.

Since I met Cassandra King at the Hoover Library Authors Conference and we decided to spend the rest of our lives together, we have written our books on opposite sides of the house. When we got married, I discovered that Sandra had never had a room of her own to write in during her entire adult life; I promised her a room with a view and all the time she needed to do her work and craft her books. She has written four novels since we met, and I believe that her new book, *Moonrise*, is the best of them. It eases my soul that I share a house with a novelist of such rare and distinctive gifts.

I know it must seem like home cooking for a husband to praise his own wife's work. But the shadow of divorce court looms over a marriage where the spouses loathe each other's work. When Sandra hands me a completed chapter or leaves it on my pillow to read, an immense joy fills me because Sandra always hands me a complete world to cast myself adrift in. In *The Sunday Wife*, she changed the English language. I've met a hundred women around the South who've whispered to me, "I used to be a Sunday wife," or "I'm still a Sunday wife; I'm married to the Bishop."

Nor can I read the last section of *The Same Sweet Girls* without breaking down at the end because I'm so touched by those amazing ties of women's friendship. I envy the tireless intimacy of women's friendship, its lastingness, and its unbendable strength. Cassandra captures all this as well as any writer producing literature today, and I love it that our house is the source of its creation.

I was present at the birth of *Moonrise*. I took Cassandra to Highlands, North Carolina, to visit my dear friend Jim Landon, who owned a lovely mountain home made holy by well-selected books and Asian art. Jim is one of those perfectly charming Southern men who dresses with distinction, decorates his home with unerring taste, makes a perfect omelet, and is one of the best lawyers in Atlanta. Cassandra fell in love with Jim immediately, as I had done when I met him in 1974. All life has more savor when Jim is around. He introduced us to his cast of immemorial friends, and hosted elegant parties on a deck that overlooks the Blue Ridge Mountains. The mountains have a clear call for certain people, and my wife was a goner for Highlands after that first week. Her novel is the product of her love affair with the high country of the South, its natives and its "summer people."

Cassandra and I have always been devotees of Daphne du Maurier's glorious book *Rebecca*. *Moonrise* is pure homage to that novel, as well as a ballad of recognition for all the strangeness and comeliness of the mountains of North Carolina. It is told in three distinct voices. It begins with an outsider, Helen Honeycutt, who is brought into a group of Highlands summer veterans who don't like it that the recently widowed Emmet Justice has married a young dietician from Florida in unseemly haste. Helen is properly terrified of the upcoming summer, when every inch of her will be reviewed and judged by some practiced Atlanta swells. The second voice is a mountain woman named Willa, who cleans and cares for all the houses. She has watched the whole strange Atlanta tribe grow up, and they have all become attached to Willa and her family. Willa adds history and perspective to her narration in the novel. By far, my favorite voice belongs to the waspy, acid tongue of Tansy Dunwoody. I perked up whenever she took to the stage because her voice can be withering and caustic, but it is always hilarious, and tender in the deepest part of her.

Cassandra loops these three voices into a stranglehold of tension as it becomes obvious that the legendary house of Moonrise means to bring great harm to the newcomer, Helen. The suspense is handled with flair and expertise, and I read the book in a single reading for that most ancient of reasons . . . to know what happened. I couldn't go to sleep until there was a sense of resolution over the fates of characters I had come to love at a mansion I'd come to fear.

Moonrise is a fabulous novel and my damn wife wrote it and that's me up there near Highlands shouting it out to the hills.

Great love . . .

On the Road Again . . . Airports,

Editors, Publicists, and

My Writing Life

|||||||||||||||

Hey, out there,

    I flew to New York on October 1 for the opening shots of my upcoming tour for *The Death of Santini*. The book comes out on October 29, when I'll be running my mouth and signing my books until I'm mercifully released to return to my writing desk to continue the writing life that has become my life. Though I far prefer writing to touring, I've always thought it was part of the contract to try with all the resources I can bring to bear to help sell the book and to give my publisher an incentive to publish my next book. Because I'm older now, travel takes a lot out of me, but my mother raised me to be a boy who likes to please, and meeting readers has given me pleasure that few writers have ever known. It's part of the business of being a writer, and I try to approach it with an open spirit and a clear-eyed understanding of how lucky I am to be asked to do it.

After arriving, I was met at the Essex House hotel the following morning by Todd Doughty, who has served as my publicist for the last three books. Over my career I've come to revere the work of publicists, and the charming Todd Doughty is exemplary of the breed. Their work is backbreaking and constant and, I believe, underappreciated. Very often, they are the best-looking people in a publishing house, and I've met some great beauties and handsome men in my various swings through their hallways. Editors, in general, are a plainer, more cerebral tribe, but even among this group, there are some dazzling exceptions to be found. My own editor, Nan Talese, has always walked the earth as one of those self-contained, well-composed New York beauties you catch glimpses of as you stroll down Fifth Avenue. In matters of good-lookingness, we writers are the ugliest of the bunch, and normally our appearance is akin to that of someone investigating a crime scene; though the women in

American writing keep producing world-class beauty in droves, and there are many breathtaking writers among them.

Todd had arranged five interviews that day. The first was with Bob Minzesheimer, the book editor for *USA Today*, whom I'd met before and liked a lot. He has great style and looks like he could have been friends with Hemingway if they'd known each other in Paris in the twenties. Our interview was cut short when he received a phone call that Tom Clancy had died and he needed to get back to his office to write an appreciation of Tom's life for the next day's edition.

Next was a radio interview where Teresa Weaver asked questions of Fannie Flagg and me about our new books. I've long been enamored of the works of Fannie Flagg; her books have always made me howl with laughter and taught me a great deal about how Southern women think. Hell, how all women think.

At lunch, Nan Talese and I had a meal brought in from the Random House cafeteria. Nan and I have been a team for over thirty years now, and I was present the night she received the first Maxwell E. Perkins Award for lifetime achievement in editing. It was a proud night for both of us. I've worked with some of the great editors of my time during my career, beginning with Shannon Ravenel, one of the founders of Algonquin Books, who passed me on to Anne Barnett, who passed me to the superb Jonathan Galassi, who has enjoyed one of the most successful careers in the history of publishing and whose departure left me in the able hands of Nan Talese. I don't think that a writer and an editor have ever been so mismatched, yet made it work out in our own ways. In her elegance, I'm always somewhat of an aardvark in her presence. She wears Armani with an unmatchable grace while I wear L.L.Bean only for dress-up occasions. Her husband, Gay Talese, writes a prose so impeccable that I find myself studying it between books. His suits are so perfect that they look woven from pelts of manatees. Together, Nan and Gay look like café society taken to its highest register.

Nan and I were there to talk about my new book, *The Death of Santini*, but I wanted to know what her other writers were doing. She always provides fresh news of Margaret Atwood and Ian McEwan, and I wanted to hear everything about her writer Valerie Martin, whose book *The Ghost of the Mary Celeste* I had just read and admired. Because we've spent thirty years together, we wander back and forth in time. Editors and reps and bookstore owners we have known together. We still remember the editorial assistants using typewriters, and when tons of people smoked in the sanctity of their own offices. But we've always agreed that it's the beauty and power and skillful use of the language that will sell a book—no matter what it is printed on. She's found great happiness on a farm she bought several years ago in Connecticut. I wondered how long our relationship could last, but I was proud of the things we had accomplished together. Looking back, I wish I had not been so sullen and cantankerous when we were editing my books, and good God, I wish I'd been better dressed as I met them at their table at Elaine's.

Great love . . .

A Long-Lasting Friendship

||||||||||||

CHARLIE GIBSON OF

GOOD MORNING AMERICA

OCTOBER 27, 2013

Hey, out there,
It is a day before my sixty-eighth birth-day and I ready myself for life on the road, which I'm too edgy and tired-blooded to do as I did with pleasure in my misspent youth. When I was in New York, I taped an interview with Charlie Gibson for *Good Morning America*. Charlie has always struck me as a man of exceptional qualities. Because he is a creature of television, I fell in love with his looks and spirit long before I got to know him. The most difficult thing for a television reporter or anchor to suggest to an audience is authenticity. Charlie's body

language speaks a truth that can't be faked or polished up or improved with time. It's a natural gift and
Charlie was born to his naturalness and it's the rarest
gift of the famous.

When *Beach Music* came out in 1995, Charlie and
his crew (also delightful) came to my house on Fripp
Island in South Carolina. I have a small addiction to
showing off the beauty of the Lowcountry, its white-
sand beaches and its green mileage of marshlands, and
Charlie's enthusiasm matches his integrity. When we
first met, he told me he thought I'd been influenced
by John Irving and I told him about *Garp* thundering
into my life and letting me know that I wasn't being
brave enough as a writer. It was a splendid literary
appraisal and let me know that Charlie Gibson was
a serious and thoughtful reader, as well as one of the
greatest students of politics I'd ever met.

New York is a city abloom with secret studios.
They exist in buildings without style or architectural
merit, but I met Charlie at one of them for a seven-
in-the-evening taping. In his elegance, he has become
handsomer as an older man than he was in his twenties. We embraced when we saw each other and he's
the only anchor I've ever hugged on a regular basis.
It's an emotional war between my Citadel and his

Princeton, but he's an affectionate, easygoing guy and I've taken advantage of that. At one meeting, he told me that he'd met everyone in the world for five minutes, but then often never saw them again. He was an aficionado of five-minute friendships. If we'd lived next door to each other I think we'd have been best friends for life. But he was incising his name into the history of American news and I was trying to write those books of mine. The interview moved me. Charlie moved me, as he always does. Once, I saw him treat two black high school girls as if they were royalty when they recognized him on a ferryboat in the Savannah River. Not every famous man or woman treats strangers with such openhearted wonder as Charlie Gibson. His interview with me was superb. Gibsonian. Deep. It airs on Tuesday, October 29.

I am lucky to get to know a man as fine as Charlie Gibson. America is lucky to have him delivering its news.

Doubleday had me staying at the Essex House hotel on Central Park South. When I was a younger and nimbler man I used to love walking the streets of New York for hours at a time, but neuropathy has slowed me up. I did walk over to Rizzoli's bookstore on Fifty-eighth Street because I have cherished the atmosphere of that store since I first arrived in New York City in 1972. I bought the new Donna Tartt book (which I've heard the best things about on earth), and the new Marisha Pessl, because I'd found myself overpowered by her prose style in her novel *Special Topics in Calamity Physics*. Also, I picked up the new novel by Bob Shacochis, *The Woman Who Lost Her Soul*. I'd revered his early short stories and did not know about his new work of fiction. As I was checking out with my credit card, a young black woman looked at my name and said, "There's a writer that goes by this name."

Once, I tried to make jokes about it and said I'd heard about the guy and understood that he was a talentless jerk. But painful experience has taught me that confession is good for the soul and certainly the most polite way of handling an awkward situation.

"Yes, ma'am. I'm that guy," I admitted.

"Ma'am? You *are* from South Carolina. I'm from Saint George."

"No, you're not. Nobody's from Saint George," I said.

"You don't even know where Saint George is," she challenged.

I laughed and said, "For four straight years, I

played for the city of Beaufort in the Saint George Tournament, which was the state championship for all towns in the state. One year, Columbia beat us by two points in the championship."

She was so excited, she did what all South Carolinians do when they meet on the road. She came out and we hugged and exchanged addresses. Then she told me she was a working poet and ran into her office to print out her poetry. Her name was Leonore Tucker and her poetry was skillful and artfully expressed. I think that Leonore Tucker may have a bright future in poetry. But it is the accidents of the road, the unplannable encounters, that I always have loved best. South Carolina is not a state; it is a cult.

Great love . . .

Vietnam Still Haunting Me . . .

||||||||||||||

Hey, out there,

When I was in New York two weeks ago, I received word that my Citadel classmate Ted Bridis had died. The news of his death shocked me on several levels. While we were at The Citadel, Ted and I were both "jocks," a despised underworld in the Corps of Cadets at that time, and it may still be so at a lower level in that rough world. Ted played football and ran track and had one of those lean, elegant bodies that trackmen wear with such ease. In memory, he was a wide receiver on the football team, but I could be wrong about that. We were mess-hall friends and we'd stop to talk every time we saw each other on campus. The Citadel was a small college and remains so, and I will always think these small places are richer in intimacy and shared experience than the universities.

After we graduated, I began my life as a draft dodger and antiwar activist while my entire class walked off that stage and stepped directly into the Vietnam War. When I talk to Ivy Leaguers or war resisters of that era, I always tell them that Vietnam was not theoretical to me, but deeply and agonizingly painful. Eight of my Citadel classmates died in that war, and three of them—Bruce Welge, Fred Carter, and Dick O'Keefe—were boys that I loved and whose friendship I cherished. Two of the managers of my basketball team died there, and my teammate Al Krobuth was a prisoner of war in one of those soul-degrading camps where our captured airmen were tortured and debased on a daily basis. I played high school baseball with Jimmy Melvin, who died on a patrol in Vietnam, and attended the funerals of Marines whose children I taught at Beaufort High School. My father served two tours of duty in Vietnam, and I adopted and raised two daughters whose father, Captain J.

W. Jones, was killed while flying close air support in defense of his Marines on the ground. I never was good at developing theories against the war, because too many slain and wounded faces rise up to argue with me about how I conducted myself during the war. I know all the excuses I used at the time, but I find myself wordless when I visit the Vietnam Veterans Memorial in Washington.

But Ted Bridis represented something about Vietnam that was agonizing to me. I had lost all contact with Ted until I was walking up to my tenth Citadel reunion with Saundra Hardin, and I heard a voice calling to me at the bottom of the stairs leading up to the Hibernian Hall. I'd not be invited back to a reunion for twenty-five years, because the appearance of *The Lords of Discipline* was on the horizon. But on that night, I heard a familiar voice call, "Hey, Pat, could you lend me a hand?"

I turned around and saw Ted Bridis for the first time since graduation. He was holding up his wheelchair in one strong arm, and asked if I'd carry it to the top steps of the Hibernian for him. In Vietnam, he had stepped on a land mine and lost both legs and an arm. The moment shocked me because I had not heard of the severity of his injuries.

"Sure, Ted. Be happy to," I said, leaning down and giving him a hug.

Then I watched as Ted Bridis crawled and struggled up those stairs, refusing the help of any of his classmates who ran to his aid.

That night I learned that he'd come close to dying on the battlefield, but was saved by the swiftness and courage of a helicopter pilot, then airlifted to the surgeons who managed to save his life. At first he seemed a deformed shell of his former self, but as we spoke that night, I realized his wounds had enhanced his manhood and his own sense of himself.

He had married a woman who was equal to his valor, and her dedication in watching over him moved me at that last dance I attended as a Citadel graduate. From my classmates, I learned that Ted had lost his Citadel ring when his arm was blown off in Vietnam. My class had collected money and presented him with a new Citadel ring, but I did not get word and failed to contribute a single dime. Ted Bridis began his long term as symbol of the Class of '67—the kind of man The Citadel could produce at its best.

Our friendship was never close, and that grieves me at this moment. But he and his wife attended every book signing I ever had in Miami, Florida. He would wait near the end of the line and I'd be furious at him for not just coming to the front to get his books signed before everyone else.

"I like waiting my turn, Pat," Ted said. "I like to hear what everybody's saying about your books. I tell them we were classmates at The Citadel."

Ted only asked me for a single thing in his life, and I have reason to believe I didn't come through on a promise I made him. He called me after Hurricane Andrew devastated his Miami home and told me that every one of my first-edition books I had signed to him was destroyed in the storm; he wanted to know if I could help replace them. I was living in San Francisco at the time and not in good emotional shape, but I started collecting my books from antiquarian bookstores and soon had every one of them except my first, *The Boo*. It was one of his prized possessions, but I could not find one for less than three thousand dollars and the Internet was not in existence.

Finally, The Boo himself found a copy in Charleston. I gathered the books together, put them in a box, addressed it, then went diving into one of the worst depressions of my life. Though I've gone over this sequence a hundred times since I heard of Ted Bridis's death, I can't remember mailing that box to Ted. I'm afraid I didn't, and I find it disgraceful.

Ted lived an exemplary life in Miami. He participated in the Paralympic Games and won many championship medals. He became an indispensable counselor to those men and women who were grievously wounded in the Afghanistan and Iraq wars. He was beloved by his classmates at The Citadel. The Boo signed his last copy of *The Boo* "To Ted Bridis, the best lamb in my sorry flock."

When I heard about his death, I remembered his voice on that Charleston night: "Hey, Pat, could you lend me a hand?"

I carried his wheelchair up the Hibernian steps, but I wish I'd done a whole lot more.

Great love . . .

The Teachers of My Life

||||||||||||

MARCH 9, 2014

Hey, out there,

I've returned to Beaufort after my long tour for *The Death of Santini*, and the town has never seemed more welcoming or restful to me. Though I feel hollowed out and exhausted by the whirlwind nature of an American book tour, I'm smart enough to know that it's still a grand way for any writer to connect to those readers he has picked up along the way. If any writer in this country has collected as fine and passionate a group of readers as I have, they're fortunate and lucky beyond anyone's imagination. It remains a shock to me that I've had a successful writing career. Not someone like me; Lord, there were too many forces working against me, too many dark currents pushing against me, but it somehow worked. Though I wish I'd written a lot more, been bolder with my talent, more forgiving of my weaknesses, I've managed to draw a magic audience into my circle. They come to my signings to tell me stories, their stories. The ones that have hurt them and made their nights long and their lives harder.

My past life rises up to greet me. Military brats that I went to school with forty years ago ask me if I remember my fourth-grade nun. Yes, that was Sister Virginia Mary, and Father James Howard was our priest, and I served my first mass after both of them made sure I'd memorized my Latin responses.

Citadel graduates show up everywhere, and, of course, I took off on this tour in October, forgetting my Citadel ring on the untidy desk where I left it. "Where's your ring?" The question always comes. My explanation always sounds hollow, but they bring their wives, children, and grandchildren to meet me. The Marines and their families show up, and military brats by the score. Teachers come by the dozens from Minneapolis to Miami.

Ah, yes, the teachers of America. When I meet

them I always say, "God's work, but not God's pay." I enrolled myself in their ranks when I wrote my book *The Water Is Wide,* and they have never issued me my walking papers. I thought I was going to be a high school English teacher in Beaufort for my entire life—that, and write execrable poetry on the side. That was my original intention, but my life and my character intervened and I never taught again in my life. In the early years I thought I would teach writing in some college in the South, but the right opportunity never presented itself. Though I've never met a teacher who was not happy in retirement, I rarely meet one who thinks that their teaching life was not a grand way to spend a human life. The unhappy ones are the young ones, those who must teach in public schools when the whole nation seems at war with the very essence of teaching.

"Why do we hate our teachers in this country?" I ask them, and not one of them disagrees with me from Santa Fe to Charleston, from New Orleans to Philadelphia.

"I don't know why. But I agree with you," the teachers say in an almost unanimous voice.

The teachers of my life saved my life and sent me out prepared for whatever life I was meant to lead.

Like everyone else, I had some bad ones and mediocre ones, but I never had one that I thought was holding me back because of idleness or thoughtlessness. They spent their lives with the likes of me and I felt safe during the time they spent with me. The best of them made me want to be just like them. I wanted young kids to look at me the way I looked at the teachers who loved me. Loving them was not difficult for a boy like me. They lit a path for me, and one that I followed with joy.

Teaching is an art form, pure and simple. I'll trust a teacher over a bureaucrat every single time—a teacher over an administrator. Education by test scores seems like the worst thing that's ever happened to American education, by far. I met ten high school English teachers on my trip whom I'd have loved to have teach me. To my surprise, my novel *The Lords of Discipline* is taught in more high school English classes than any of my others. I thought the language of the barracks and the nasty racism of the Corps would prevent that book from ever being taught in an American classroom. I met a whole cadre of teachers in Kansas City, Missouri, who had taught *The Lords of Discipline* for years. When I asked the head of the English department at a large public high school how his teachers navigate through parents and school boards offended by the book, he told me it had been a challenge, indeed. His teachers let their students make the case with the school board, and the passion of those students had carried the day each time the subject had come up. I fell in love with the English teachers of Kansas City, and that is a bond that'll never be broken.

Yet the unhappiness of teachers was a constant theme, and they suffer from the lack of respect and honor due them for their choice to spend their lives teaching the children that are sent to them. The testing of American children all began with well-meaningness and high-mindedness. "No Child Left Behind" is a phrase of enormous beauty, yet it has caused more suffering among teachers than the pitiful wages we pay them. Whether it's a Republican or Democratic administration doesn't seem to make a scintilla of difference. The theories that are born in Washington, D.C., and in the Ivy League are ascendant throughout the country, and as far as I can tell and as well as I can listen, they've had a chilling effect on most of the classrooms in our land. A nation of unhappy teachers makes for a sadder and more endangered America.

Before my beloved English teacher Gene Norris died, he was given a lifetime achievement award by the South Carolina Council of Teachers of English. The year before, Gene had received the first "Guiding Spirit" Award, given by the Thomas Wolfe Society to honor Margaret Roberts, the extraordinary woman who had taught high school English to the great novelist. It was a good year for Gene, even though he was suffering greatly from the leukemia that would kill him. We drove to Greenville together for the ceremony on one of our last road trips. The chemo had made Gene grouchy and dyspeptic, and he said to me, "I don't want you to go on and on about me. The way you usually do. You always exaggerate my influence on you. I'm so tired of you gilding the lily. I told them I don't want this award and I certainly don't deserve it."

"Then why am I wasting my valuable time driving you to Greenville?" I asked.

"Because it's good for teachers, carpetbagger. It's good for all teachers—everywhere. They don't get much," he said, and he was grinning. "But I'm going to walk out of there if you do your usual bullshit about me."

"I'll say anything I want. I'm an American. I've got rights."

Gene was magnificent when he received the award, and I was not the only one who saw him cry that day. Afterward, we were together when two bright and hilarious teachers stood up later in the program.

The first said, "No child left behind."

"Every child left behind," the second said.

"No school left behind," the first said.

"Every school left behind," the second said.

"No teacher left behind?" asked the first.

"Every damn teacher left behind."

Gene and I joined in the standing ovation for these two singular women. On the way home, Gene was reflective and still deeply moved by the ceremony.

"I've had an amazing life, Pat. I wouldn't change a thing. Except this: they used to trust teachers with the kids they sent us. It's all different now and oh, so wrong."

So the teachers came to my signings as they always do. Some were veterans of the inner-city schools and their voices filled up with urgency and despair. Some were in danger of being fired because of the low test scores of the students at their schools. When I asked a white woman in Philadelphia if she ever thought about transferring to a suburban school, she bristled at me. "Why would I do that? My kids need me. I'm in love with them. Who'd fight for them if it weren't for teachers like me?"

Teaching remains a heroic act to me, and teachers live a necessary and all-important life. We are killing their spirit with unnecessary pressure and expectations that seem forced and destructive to me. Long ago I was one of them. I still regret I was forced to leave them. My entire body of work is because of men and women like them.

———

The word "blog" is the ugliest word in the English language to me. But I've written in journals in a haphazard fashion since I was a young writer. The journal I keep now is the material that makes up my own "blog"—though I've no idea what a blog is supposed to do or what it is supposed to consist of. Why it appeals to anyone is mysterious to me. But I use it as a way to sneak back into my own writing without being noticed. A new novel awaits my arrival, prepares for my careful inspection. Yet a novel is always a long dream that lives in me for years before I know where to go to hunt it out. When I found myself in new cities or strange airports on this trip, I could feel it stirring around on the outer rings of consciousness. I could feel it begin to layer itself. Though it pointed to no real beginnings or endings, I believe I've got two long novels and three short ones still in me. But my health has to cooperate and I need to pay more attention to my health. It is not long life I wish for—it is to complete what I have to say about the world I found around me from boyhood to old age. Because I've gotten older, I worry that there will be a steep decline in my talent, but I promise not to let the same thing happen to my passion for writing.

My career still strikes me as miraculous. That a boy raised on Marine bases in the South, taught by Roman Catholic nuns in backwater Southern towns that loathed Catholics, and completed his education with an immersion into The Citadel—the whole story sounds fabricated, impossible even to me. Maybe especially to me.

Throughout my career I've lived in constant fear that I wouldn't be good enough, that I'd have nothing to say, that I'd be laughed at, humiliated—and I'm old enough to know that fear will follow me to the very last word I'll ever write.

As for now, I feel the first itch of the novel I'm supposed to write—the grain of sand that irritates the soft tissues of the oyster. The beginning of the world as I don't quite know it. But I trust I'll begin to know it soon.

Great love . . .

Barbara Warley Was Loved
by Everyone

||||||||||||||

I've come to that point in my life when my memories seem as important as the life I'm now leading. On February 26, I drove from Beaufort, South Carolina, to Williamsburg, Virginia, to attend the memorial service of Barbara Nelson Warley—she of the grand spirit and radiant beauty. Her husband, John, who roomed with me on the baseball team, was the best friend I made at The Citadel, and we were inseparable during our senior year. Neither of us dated much that year—no, let me be blunter than that; we dated hardly at all, except on big weekends when cadets in Romeo and Tango companies had sisters who required escorts to the Corps Day Hop. But John and I would drive around Charleston on weekend nights, talking about girls and where we might go to pick some of them up. We never found that mythical place.

In Rome, at dinner with the novelist Gore Vidal, I once talked about my friendship with John Warley. Gore was fascinated by military colleges and had liked my book *The Lords of Discipline*. His father had attended West Point and had been a legendary football player there.

"You do realize, Pat, that Mr. Warley and you were gay."

"I can't wait to tell John," I said.

I missed John and Barbara's wedding at the National Cathedral in Washington. I believe I was embroiled in a fight with the school board to get my job back on Daufuskie Island, and I did not meet Barbara until after *The Water Is Wide* was published. They were living in the Claremont Apartments, within rock-throwing distance from the Culpeper Street house I lived in when Dad was stationed at the Pentagon.

Barbara Warley was a pure knockout, the stuff bad novels are made of. I'd never seen such a pretty girl and I found myself as intimidated as I was dazzled. But she bounced up to me and kissed me on the lips and said, "John's told me all about you and I bet we're friends forever."

So it was and so it would always be. When John went to work the next day, Barbara and I began telling each other the stories of our lives. Instinctively, we identified ourselves as members of that unhappy tribe who come from troubled and deeply flawed families. Like me, she endured one of those violent fathers who made their kid's life a march of shame and terror. I had begun to write the first chapters of *The Great Santini* and told her of my own difficulty in describing a father I had loathed since I was an infant. When I told her I'd always worried that John's parents did not seem to like me very much, she surprised me by saying that I was John's parents' least liked friend among all of John's acquaintances. With a great laugh, she then admitted that John's mother and father didn't seem to like her much better. Barbara thought the Warleys thought John would marry a much higher-class girl, "and they certainly want John hanging around with a much higher-class guy than you."

We would be fast friends for over forty years. I've

had a bad tendency to fall in love with my friends' wives, but it would seem unnatural not to fall for Barbara Warley. Everyone came under her spell, male and female, and it was a lemon-like soul who could resist her sweetness and vitality. She and John made a great marriage out of it and produced four children for the ages. No one writes much about the joy other people's children bring to your life, but Caldwell, Nelson, Mary Beth, and Carter have delighted me each time our paths have crossed. Mary Beth was a Korean orphan, adopted by John and Barbara, who provided some kind of ripeness and deepening of the whole family. John was a successful lawyer in Newport News, Virginia, and a local player in Republican politics. Then he and Barbara announced that John was selling his law firm and moving to San Miguel de Allende in Mexico. John also told me he planned to become a novelist.

This was akin to me calling John Warley to tell him I was becoming an astronaut. But Mexico was their destiny as a family, and San Miguel changed everything about them and became the most romantic adventure of their lives.

On their trips back and forth between Mexico and Virginia, they would always stop for a couple of days' rest at my house on Fripp Island. This was the time when my friendship with John deepened again and Barbara would tell me about Mexico in a rapturous trance. Now she was wearing Mexican jewelry and clothes, and everything about her life in San Miguel seemed meaningful and backlit with wonder. John and I would talk about novels and writing, and he was doing some serious work. His prose style was becoming a lovely and serious thing.

Eventually, the Warleys returned to Richmond for John to resume practicing law. Like most writers, he had discovered it was easier to make a living doing something besides writing novels. It was during their time in Richmond that tragedy struck and Barbara found out she had breast cancer; an aggressive chemotherapy treatment eradicated the cancer but destroyed her joints, and she was to suffer debilitating pain for the rest of her life.

When I called Barbara when she returned to her house to recover, I didn't know what to say to her. Breast cancer seems so cruel and disfiguring to me, something soul-killing and personal. Being pretty had always been such a part of who Barbara was; I wanted to say something to let her know that the cancer had not touched her singular beauty.

"Hey, Barbara, you okay, kid?" I said.

"I'm hanging in there, darling," Barbara answered.

"I still get horny when I hear your voice," I said, instantly horrified with myself.

She saved me by laughing hard enough for it to hurt.

"It's just like you, Conroy," she said. "All talk and no action."

After John retired from the law, they moved to Beaufort, and Cassandra and I saw the Warleys a lot as a couple. Everyone who met them in Beaufort was swept away by Barbara's charm and comeliness. John finished his novel *A Southern Girl*, which proves that his late call to novel writing was a path well chosen. It is a brilliant literary achievement and the first in a series of novels published by Story River Books of the University of South Carolina Press. It is a novel that soars and moves with a lyrical sweep that is rare in modern fiction. I wish I had written it.

Four days before Barbara died, I attended the wedding of Caldwell Warley to the comely Vanessa Snyder at the Summerall Chapel at The Citadel. Barbara and John had returned to Mexico for the past two years and his reports of her condition had worried me. When her son Nelson walked the mother of the groom down the aisle, I turned to see Barbara Warley, the girl I'd loved for forty years. She looked frail and thin and unsteady to me, but there was an intake of breath from the crowd as this gorgeous woman was led up the aisle by her good-looking son Nelson. God, she was beautiful.

At a crowded and boisterous reception on Daniel Island, I went through the crowd looking for her and I stumbled into her looking for me. We fell into each other's arms as we always did. She kissed me on the lips and then wiped her lipstick off with her hand. We hugged again and held each other tight.

"I still get horny when I see you, Barbara," I said.

"Oh, Conroy. All talk and no action."

And both of us laughed. The last words we'd ever say to each other.

Barbara took her own life at her son Carter's house in Williamsburg later that week. The pain had gotten overwhelming, and no one I met at the memorial service displayed the slightest bit of anger at the way she ended her life. Her children were devastated and her friends wept. A group flew up from Mexico. Mary Beth was near total collapse. I cried every time I held one of her kids. I met all her friends from Virginia. The speeches in her honor were all moving and killing at the same time.

When I got home, it was announced among our Citadel classmates: "John Warley's wife died last week. Barbara Warley—loved by everyone."

How George R. R. Martin Made Me
Love Dire Wolves, Giants, Dwarves,
and Dragons . . .

‖‖‖‖‖‖‖‖‖‖‖

Hey, out there,

When I returned home to Beaufort after my book tour was over, I brought part of the tour back to my house with me. I've never found myself attracted to the world of fantasy writing, with a few quite notable exceptions. When I lived in Italy, I came under the sway of Italo Calvino and his books. *The Baron in the Trees, The Cloven Viscount, If on a Winter's Night a Traveler,* and especially *Invisible Cities* sparked deep mysteries in me. At the same time, I became familiar with the nearly unclassifiable work of Jonathan Carroll, who has a narrative voice that can take me places I never knew I needed to go. Ursula Le Guin and Ray Bradbury have brought me many great pleasures, and I've tried to read as many of the fairy tales of world literature as I can. The Arthurian legends have always found a captive audience with me; I read *The Once and Future King* and few books have ever struck me with the powers of its wondrous imagination. I read it recently and failed to cherish it as I once did, and I asked myself if something squirrelly and unappreciative had entered my reading life as I've grown older.

I've never relished the company of the dystopian novel much, but then I remember Margaret Atwood's *The Handmaid's Tale*, and that was good enough to shut my mouth for a while. Though I revere much of the writing of Cormac McCarthy, he did not seduce me with *The Road*. Literary taste is a defining thing in all of us. It is as unpredictable as it is fascinating. I'm as astonished by the work of Jonathan Franzen as I am incapable of reading five pages of Thomas Pynchon. I treasure the works of John Fowles and Ian McEwan and I want to like Martin Amis, but just can't or don't. Metafiction sends me running to the hills and always makes me think that I'm not smart enough to understand it. I'm confident enough in myself as a reader to think, *If I can't understand it, then who the hell can?* The pleasure principle kicks into high gear whenever I pick up a book. Toni Morrison's prose style is a joy-inducing mastery of the language, and no one deserves a Nobel Prize more than Alice Munro. Philip Roth is a gift to American letters, but the most celebrated book of the eighties, *Infinite Jest* by David Foster Wallace, left me feeling like a beast of burden as I slogged my way toward that infinite finish line. A. S. Byatt's book *Possession* grabbed me by the throat and held me in its immense thrall until the very end. I hated everything about J. M. Coetzee's book *Disgrace,* but could not deny its power and greatness when I completed it. Anne Rivers Siddons's *Colony* made me fall in love with Maine, and she's the most Southern woman I've ever met. Ron Rash's *Serena* made me think about the North Carolina mountains in a way that Thomas Wolfe never did.

I believe I could write like this forever and not remember half the books that made my time on earth so wonderful. The reading of great books has been a life-altering activity to me and, for better or worse, brought me singing and language-obsessed to that country where I make my living. Except for teaching, I've had no other ambition in life than to write books that mattered.

All of this is preamble to the fact that I met the most extraordinary American writer while I was in the middle of my tour. His name is George R. R. Martin and I think he is a writer for the ages. Over the past several years, I've kept hearing about George R. R. Martin from his readers, who often verge on the edge of possession. But my own form of literary snobbism has kept me from reading him, because George writes in a field I encounter with much resistance—he writes in the genre of fantasy, part of the lower pastures of world fiction. Despite my love of Tolkien, Italo Calvino, Jonathan Carroll, and Ursula Le Guin, I like to spend my reading time among other writers. I had also known personally one of the great fantasy writers of our time, Robert Jordan, which was the pen name for Jim Rigney Jr., a Citadel graduate who got his degree seven years after I did. Jim and I were taught by the same distinguished English teachers at The Citadel, and he blazed an amazing trail with his Wheel of Time series that led some to refer to him as the new Tolkien. I read several books in the series, enjoyed them, but never found myself captured by

Jim's world of fantasy. Yet Jim's books became number one bestsellers on the *New York Times* bestseller list every time he came out with a new volume. He died of a very extreme form of cancer in the middle of his prime. But his fantasy required a leap of the imagination I was not prepared to give at that time of my life, and I've regretted it. The last time I met him I asked him if he knew any other college that had produced two writers who had occupied the number one slot on the *NYT* list. It seemed a rare distinction. A week later he called me and said he'd researched my question and only Harvard had produced more than two. Naturally it was Harvard, but for novels like *Love Story* and *Jurassic Park*—none of the Harvard heavyweights like Norman Mailer. I thought John Updike had probably made it, but Jim was too happy with his findings and I let it go.

My friend Katherine Clark was the first full-fledged fanatic of George R. R. Martin that I found and she was relentless on the subject. Katherine had published an oral biography of my friend Eugene Walter called *Milking the Moon*. It's a one-of-a-kind book that celebrates the life of a quirky unknown writer who lived a fascinating and joy-giving life. I did not meet Katherine until she introduced me before I gave a signing at Page & Palette bookstore in Fairhope, Alabama. We've been fast friends since. She is one of the few friends in my life who reads more than I do, and her eye is cunning and so far infallible. She went to Harvard, then wrote her dissertation on William Faulkner at Emory University. Our friendship is based on the books we've read and those we are now writing. Two years ago she started reading George R. R. Martin, and I listened as a fanatic was born on the telephone. By then, her good taste was a proven commodity, but I listened to her rapture with growing discomfort. She read his A Song of Ice and Fire series of five door-stopping books, then read them again to see if they were as good as she originally thought. She found them much better. She started throwing out comparisons to Dante and Shakespeare and I thought that the seafood she was eating from the BP oil spill was starting to affect her brain in Pensacola. One of the things I've admired about Katherine is that she can read books by people she hates, and if the writing is good, she will surrender her sword and admit to the book's excellence. I can do that sometimes, but not often.

"Shakespeare?" I once asked Katherine, mockery in my voice.

"Yes, Shakespeare, Pat. We read the same guy and I think this guy might be better."

"Do you tell your Harvard friends that? Or just us Citadel boys?"

"I tell all my Harvard friends that they're just like you—they haven't read him either."

"Magic, dire wolves, mammoths, giants, dwarves, and dragons. I can't believe I don't want to read these books."

"Read them. Then tell me I'm wrong," she said.

"That's a deal. If you quit talking about them," I said.

As if often does, fate crept into this conversation without either Katherine or me noticing its intrusion. When I first saw my tour schedule, I thought it had been designed by Dante Alighieri. From last October 15 to December 20, I was on the road to push my new book, *The Death of Santini.* It is part of the covenant I sign with Doubleday that I'll do everything possible to help them sell the book, including not getting drunk on tour or embarrassing my publishing company with my cutting-up on the road. I go out to sell books and it has become one of the greatest things about being a writer during my lifetime. No writer should turn down the chance of meeting the readers of his work. I went as far north as Minnesota, as far east as Philadelphia and New York, as far south as Miami, and as far west as the Missouri River. But there was one stopover that made no sense to me. In what I thought was a mistake of planning, I saw a two-day trip to Santa Fe shoehorned into the dead middle of my tour, and this seemed a couple of states too far for me. I know how daily travel wears me down after a couple of days on the road, and I had no idea why a side trip to Santa Fe was on the list. But when I called my redoubtable publicist, Todd Doughty, he explained that it was the home of George R. R. Martin and that George had recently restored an old theater in Santa Fe where he showed classic movies and interviewed authors onstage himself.

"Have you ever heard of George R. R. Martin, Pat?" Todd asked me.

"Is he a good guy, Todd?" I asked.

"He's a wonderful guy and everyone who knows him says it's true," Todd answered. "Also, he happens to love your books."

"Ah, my idea of a splendid man, myself."

Immediately, I called Katherine Clark at her home in Pensacola and said, "I'm going to meet Shakespeare."

"You're meeting George R. R. Martin in Santa Fe," she said into the phone. "I'm coming, too."

"You were not invited," I said.

"I'm coming anyway," she said.

So we did. I bought a copy of *A Game of Thrones* from Park Road Books in Charlotte and was almost finished with it when I made the first stop of my life in Santa Fe. I woke to the birdsong of an enchanted hill town that looked more European than American. It had a modest but ancient feel to it. I was staying at the Inn of the Five Graces and it was as splendid a small hotel as it could possibly be. My bathroom was a work of art, flashing in colorful shapes of Mexican tile. There were tapestries and weavings hanging from the walls. The adobe walls make the city a muted ode to the color of brown. Because I'm not a great lover of Mexican food, the cuisine of Santa Fe will never find justice with me. I do not like the meals of my city to be cilantro based. But the fault lies in me and not in Santa Fe. It is a city of a thousand art galleries. The paintings seemed both world-class and fearfully overpriced to me, and my heart does not sing when confronted by cowboy-and-Indian art. I passed by a lot of cowboys cast in bronze and a lot of Indians eyeing them with motionless disdain.

That night we met at a restaurant in Santa Fe. By this time, I had finished *A Game of Thrones* and had thought it magnificent. I sat next to George and found him charming, gregarious, unpretentious, and a complete pleasure to be around. He was so disarmingly nice that I would have expected him never to have published a haiku in his life. He dressed with unstudied simplicity and wore a Greek fisherman's hat with all the panache of a Greek fisherman. The restaurant he chose was first rate, as I knew it would be from the startling feasts he describes in such luscious detail in his books. He wears his success well, lightly threaded but perfectly made, and he's proud of this world he has created out of his own eclectic imagination. His long apprentice work in Hollywood taught him how to write great and convincing dialogue. His storytelling powers are intoxicating and pitch-perfect in their execution. We told each other some stories of our lives and we talked to the people at the table with us. George had no need to dominate, which I found wondrous to behold. His curiosity extended around the table, to the three publicists from Doubleday—Todd Doughty, Alison Rich, and Suzanne Herz—and to the hero-worshipping Katherine Clark (who could barely utter a word in her literary George R. R. thrall). He was that rare kind of celebrity—his success had not seemed to rout the best parts of his nature. His fame had not ruined the boy in him who'd once fallen in love with the fantastic worlds of comic books and science fiction. But the sentence I just wrote limits his achievement and hides it away in a bottle of lesser literary elixirs. I judge him much greater than that.

The next night, he interviewed me on the stage of the old, intimate theater he paid good money to restore. It was small and held about two hundred people at most, and he and I took up much of the stage that was barely large enough to behead the enemy of the state. George R. R. started the evening off in the most surprising way—he began to praise my own novels, especially *The Lords of Discipline* and *The Prince of Tides.* Several times he discussed my writing about The Citadel and how it influenced him when he wrote about the Northern Wall that protected the Seven Kingdoms from the barbarity of the wildings of the North. The brothers of the Night's Watch, the men of the black, reminded me of The Citadel with my college's strict codes and military purity. George R. R. remembered the black cadet at The Citadel who was helped along by my narrator, Will McLean, in *The Lords of Discipline,* and it helped shape his portrait of Samwell Tarly, the weakling and keeper of the Crows who is protected by the bastard of Winterfell, Jon Snow. Yes, I could see it and I could also catch the scent of *Lord of the Flies*. All through his work I catch the echoes of an extremely well-read man, and a man whose capacity for learning from other writers seems limitless.

Then George R. R. Martin delivered one of the great valentines of my writing life. He talked about visiting Hawaii for the first time and his wife chastising him for not looking at the spectacular coastline of Hawaii as they drove to their hotel some distance from Honolulu. He told the audience he couldn't look at that coastline because he was in the middle of reading *The Prince of Tides*.

You, out there. Listen up.

Generosity is the rarest of qualities in American writers. Before George R. R. Martin told me that in front of eyewitnesses in Santa Fe, no other writer I recall had ever told me something I'd written had influenced them. I don't think it had ever happened to me before. I've always felt a vague sense of guilt that I search for plunder and inspiration in every book or poem or story I pick up. Other people's books are treasures when stories emerge in molten ingots that a writer can shape to fit his or her own talents. Magical theft has always played an important part of my own writer's imagination.

When I first read *David Copperfield* in Joseph Monte's English class, the book took full command of my imagination and I longed to write novels in the Dickensian manner; until I was stopped in my tracks that same year by *Crime and Punishment* and *The Brothers Karamazov.* Down the road, I got Faulknered and Steinbecked, Hemingwayed and Fitzgeralded. In college I was Virginia Woolfed and dazzled by Willa Cather and became a devotee of George Eliot. I don't know when reading books became the most essential thing about me, but it happened over the years and I found myself the most willing servant of what I considered a rich habit.

A great book took me into worlds where I was never supposed to go. I met men whose lives I wished to make my own and men whom I would cheerfully kill. Great writers introduced me to women I wanted to marry and women who would make me run for my life. I was raised in a tyrant's home and my mother had thirteen pregnancies while sleeping in her oppressor's bed. Let me marry Isabel Archer in *The Portrait of a Lady* and put on my track shoes when I encounter the rise of a Lady Macbeth in my life. But literature is vast and subtle enough to make me fool enough to fall in love with its villains and scoundrels. I've a soft spot for Becky Sharp in my heart, and the dry-ice evil of Iago still manages to raise my blood pressure when I dip again into the pages of *Othello*.

I've admired the work of Don DeLillo, but never gave my heart to it, whereas John Irving found his voice and made me his devotee forever after *The World According to Garp*. When Gabriel García Márquez is good, there is no one better. I could read Richard Russo forever.

But there I go again. Even as I record this, I'm aware of a hundred writers who filled me with happiness over the years and provided countless pleasures as I read through their books and started to expand with fresh knowledge of the family of man. Some books I took on as self-improvement projects. In sixth grade, under the tutelage of Sister Nathaniel, I decided to read the entire Bible. I thought it would bring me closer to God. It took me three years to complete the project and then my mother was upset that I had read the King James version of the Bible that Grandpa Peek had given me, instead of the Douay-Rheims version that was approved by the Catholic

Church. By accident, I had read the beautiful Bible, and the magisterial rhythms of the King James version are the ones that still move through my bloodstream. In my twenties I read the four volumes of the journals of Andre Gidé and everything that Camus ever wrote. I read ten volumes of Balzac, ten by Zola, all by Colette, and I found I admired the work of Simone de Beauvoir far more than that of her strange lover, Sartre. For some reason, I'd gotten it into my head that the French held the mystery of where all knowledge lay.

So a lifetime passes and I manage to live a life quite badly. I marry three times, help raise four children, have one of them stolen from me, inherit five stepchildren, and write the books that have described both the pains and the joys I encountered living that life. Then I arrive on a stage with George R. R. Martin in Santa Fe, New Mexico, in my sixty-eighth year, and encounter a writer whose body of work is completely alien to me. I've avoided science fiction most of my life—for the simple reason that I didn't care much about it. No matter how many years Katherine Clark had championed Mr. Martin, she had revealed nothing that made me want to rush out and buy his work. Up to now, I'd cared little for the

march of imaginary kings in made-up lands of yes-
teryear. Though I'd been one of those "comic book
boys" whose heart once sang with the heroics of
action heroes, I'd grown up surrounded by Marine
Corps fighter pilots whom I thought would make out
just fine in battles with Superman and Batman and
Spider-Man and all the rest. They never quite took
me prisoner in my imagination. It might have been
my biblical reading that made me unprepared for the
comic book pantheon of heroes. I was not as afraid
of Batman beating me up when Lot's wife was being
turned into a pillar of salt for the lightweight crime of
looking back at a burning city. So I entered the world
of George R. R. Martin tentative and doubtful. But I
needed to hush Katherine Clark up, and reading the
work was the only way to do it.

So, I agreed to a compact to read *A Game of Thrones*
and nothing else if I thus desired. I had not prepared
myself for the pure genius of George R. R. Martin.
His writing is lush and beautiful and is a perfect fit
for his life's work. His entrance into this exotic and
created world of his is confident and shows no sign
of hesitation or doubt. He inhabits his world with an
ease of creation that seems impossible to imagine. His
achievement brings me to a halt—to study the many

limitations of my own imagination. The dialogue between his characters is as real and distinct as are those to be found in John le Carré or Elmore Leonard. His descriptions are first-rate and his fiery tale of the birth of dragons is fully equal, if not far more spectacular, than the resurrection of Christ in the New Testament. He writes about religion, wars and gods, men and women, mothers and children, with a pure shiningness that surpasses mere talent. Mr. Martin has to be dealt with in some serious way by the gatekeepers of American fiction. What do *The New Yorker, The New York Times, The New York Review of Books, Harper's,* and *The Atlantic* do about this guy? I'm now finished with *A Game of Thrones, A Clash of Kings, A Storm of Swords, A Feast for Crows,* and am three hundred pages into *A Dance with Dragons.* This much reading at least allows me to pour wine for the guests of the great number of his tribe of devotees he's attracted. I am 4,300 pages into the world George R. R. Martin has created, and long for 5,000 more. Do I consider it grand entertainment? I certainly do, but I also consider it literature standing on the high ground of our language. His characters spring to life on every page and I'll take Tyrion the Imp over Falstaff any day . . . take Cersei over Lady Macbeth . . . take Jon

Snow over Hamlet...take Sansa over Cordelia. Martin has created his own world and it shines with its own set of special constellations, its own comets, its unforgettable citizens, its cold immensity, its blood-thirsty battles, its score-settling by the gods and their rapacious servants among the hideous and beautiful men and women created in their passage...It's all extraordinary and unlike anything I've ever read. A Song of Ice and Fire is not like anything I've ever read before. It is American literature thrown at our feet—and for those of us in a love affair with the language, it's up to us to stretch and broaden our horizons, to bend and welcome it into the pantheon.

Great love ...

A Eulogy for a
Southern Gentleman

|||||||||||||||

APRIL 23, 2014

Here is the way it was in the city of Atlanta in 1973, over forty years ago when the dogwoods bloomed along Peachtree Road and there was a party in the Governor's Mansion in Buckhead. Barbara Conroy and I were new to the city, and an invite for a party from Jimmy and Rosalynn Carter sounded like a ticket to heaven after being run out of South Carolina. We knew no one in the city until that night, and it seemed like we knew everyone when the evening was over. As we were crowding around the doorway to the huge dining room—it was a night to celebrate the writers and journalists in Georgia—I heard the sound of high heels clicking against marble in the old tap dance of youth and radiance, and I turned to see Anne Rivers Siddons and her flashy, dapper husband by her side—that devilish boy from Saint Albans, the one with that ironical smile he perfected while at Princeton—and he was laughing about something that Annie was saying as they made their brilliant entrance into the heart of things.

They were beautiful to look at. Annie was as pretty and sexy a woman as ever drew breath in the sweet air of Georgia, and Heyward symbolized some essence of the Atlanta businessman—sharp, tailored, and successful, every inch of him finely wrought, brimming with the innate class of the Eastern establishment. To me, this is what I wanted Atlanta to look like— these were the people I'd moved to the city to meet. This was the night I met the writers Paul Darcy Boles, Paul Hemphill, Jim Townsend, Larry Wood, Joe Cummings, Betsy Fancher, Terry Kay, and so many more, people I would come to love over the years. By all accounts, it was a magnificent gathering, except that alcohol was forbidden to be served in the Governor's Mansion during the Carter years. Toward the end, the sound of various writers choking and clawing at their throats was heard around the dining room as the first stages of delirium tremens began to set in at the tables to our right and left.

So that was how it began on a tender spring day in Atlanta, and now it has ended in one of the tenderest springs in the memory of Charleston. I was too young to understand then that the brisk sound of high heels tapping out a rhythmic clatter on Georgia marble would result in a friendship that would last for forty years, that would open up my heart in so many ways I didn't know it could be opened, and that my life had changed forever by this couple born into it at that very moment.

Here is how Heyward and Annie struck me then and strike me now; time has done nothing to change what I feel about them both. They had sprung alive from the pages of an F. Scott Fitzgerald short story. Heyward was shy about revealing his privileged, Ivy League background, and I believe it took over five seconds for him to tell me he was a Princeton graduate that night. In the next four thousand meetings we enjoyed, Heyward would dip into his high-stepping past and remind me that he had gone to Princeton

while I had spent the majority of my youth major-
ing in "flamethrowers and bazookas" at The Citadel. It was an article of faith in our relationship that
Heyward believed he had received a better college
education than I did. It got so bad that I would enter
an Atlanta party, spot Heyward in the corner with
Annie, and I'd say, "Hey, Heyward. Tell me now that
you went to Princeton so you don't have to drop it
later." I'd then hug both of them, and find out what
was going on in their very well-lived lives. It assured
me that I'd always have my first drink of the night
while talking to Annie and Heyward.

My association of them with F. Scott Fitzgerald was
not accidental. Heyward, in his understated elegance
and good taste, had fallen in love with Anne Rivers,
who was about to begin a career that would make her
a household name among discriminating readers in
America. By marrying Heyward, Annie had placed
her destiny alongside one of the greatest readers she
would ever encounter, her head cheerleader during her remarkable career as the queen of Southern
fiction, whose passionate love of her work was just
another side to the most successful literary marriage
it's been my pleasure to observe. Heyward became her
number one fan, first reader, first editor, first critic,

and the first to tell Annie that what she'd written was original, unique, and even magical. Heyward Siddons found great joy in telling me that he had married the most beautiful prose style in the South. Here is what was remarkable about Heyward Siddons, the Princetonian: he knew it, supported his wife in every way conceivable, and would shout it aloud to the world. He was the first great male feminist I ever met. He made his life a conscious celebration of his wife's career. Heyward Siddons made it all possible, and he made it look effortless.

It was not lost on me that Anne Rivers Siddons was some wraithlike incarnation of that lost soul of American letters, Zelda Fitzgerald. But where her husband, Scott, was enormously jealous of his wife's talent, Heyward held his hand over Annie's, realizing its precious flame. It was never easy for women writers in America, and it was especially not easy in 1973. The legendary editor Jim Townsend dismissed Annie's writing as mere "froufrou" when I came to Atlanta. Women were held back, not listened to; given the lightest stories to report; and never given the chance to walk as equals in the boys' club of Atlanta writers. As Heyward announced to me my first year in Atlanta, Annie was about to change all that, and change it she did. It was Heyward who gave me my first warning of incoming fire when *Heartbreak Hotel* was published. "It'll define Southern college life in the 1950s, Conroy, the way Fitzgerald described Princeton of the twenties," and it did.

Annie then embarked on a many-pillared career that lifted off into the stratosphere . . . *Peachtree Road, Gone with the Wind*'s successor as *the* Atlanta novel; *Downtown*, Annie's rendition of the civil rights movement in Atlanta, including a grand portrayal of Jim Townsend. *Fox's Earth, Colony, Homeplace* came off her typewriter with astonishing speed, proving that hers was a deep, profligate talent that was not bound by any singular geography. Heyward Siddons played policeman, watchdog, and was the furious protector of her privacy as Annie wrote the books that would change our times.

Their house on Vermont Road served as a pleasure palace for the writers of Atlanta. Heyward and Annie hosted dinner parties that still feel like some of the best parts of my young manhood. Heyward was a refined, articulate host who wrote book reviews for *Atlanta* magazine, read *The New York Times* daily, kept up with the news of the world and literature, kept alive the curiosity he developed in his early career in television and radio, could charm your socks off (on the rare occasions I wore socks), and turn his sardonic, or should I say satanic, wit on anyone who popped into his news-finder on any particular night. He had a special genius for ferreting out any bad review I had received throughout our great land and cheerfully reciting from it as we dined over one of Annie's shrimp casseroles. You had to be fast on your feet to be a worthy guest at Heyward Siddons's house. Those conversations sparkled in the Atlanta air.

Remember the click of Annie's high heels coming around that corner of the Governor's Mansion? I've been following the dance of that pretty woman and her debonair husband for forty years now. I followed them from Atlanta to a writers' weekend in Tate Mountain, Georgia, to the mansion South of Broad, to a wedding in Rome, and to the deep immortal silences of the Maine coast. For me, the great, unseeable reward I received from the marriage of Heyward and Annie Siddons is to have been a witness to the greatest love story it has been my privilege to watch. This couple found each other in Atlanta during a time of stormy change in the South. That woman with the tapping heels found a man who did an elegant soft-shoe beside her in a dance that would last the rest of their lives. If Heyward and Annie ever fought, I was never a witness to it. If they were ever furious with me or anyone else, I never knew of it. They seemed inseparable to me, and I rarely saw them when they weren't together, a perfect match, a bindery of souls. They taught every writer they ever met the limits of marriage and came close to proving it had no limits. Heyward Siddons taught all the male writers in his life how to treat a woman, how to love a wife, how to live a life that was joyful and rich with happiness and worthy of imitation. Unlike F. Scott Fitzgerald, Heyward, you lived a full life with stalwart sons, lovely grandchildren, and a remarkable body of friends.

There were no madhouses or crack-ups, and you let your Zelda bloom into one of the most storied careers ever lived by a woman in the American South. You made that possible, Heyward, and through Annie's work you helped launch the careers of Josephine Humphreys, Patti Callahan Henry, Cassandra King, Mary Alice Monroe, Sue Monk Kidd, Dorothea Benton Frank, Rebecca Wells, and hundreds of others like them. A writer has never found a better man to accompany her on her waltz toward art. Every writer

needs the solid foundation of the love and ground-
ing you brought to Annie's life. And in your generosity, you gave it to the whole generation of writers
who came to adore you, and that is your legacy for all
time—until our last words are written.

Remembering an
Irreplaceable Friend

||||||||||||||

NOVEMBER 8, 2014

Among the worst things about growing old is the loss of those irreplaceable friends who added richness and depth to your life. I met Tim Belk in Beaufort in 1967, the first year I taught and coached at Beaufort High School. We were the only guests at a dinner that the only writer in Beaufort, Ann Head, had put together so we could meet and form what she was certain would become a serious "literary" friendship. Ann had taught me creative writing my senior year in high school and had written me a series of generous-spirited letters about the sadsack poems I wrote for the literary magazine at The

Citadel. Ann Head and my father hated each other on sight, and she worried that my college was the worst possible breeding ground for a young man who wished to be a novelist. Ann's articulate response to the shaping of my writing life by my father and The Citadel was my introduction to Tim Belk. With this, Ann Head made my life delicious and presented me with a friend who would prove a treasury of constant delight. Tim Belk became a dreamboat of a friend, and the news of his death in San Francisco this October killed something of measureless value inside of me and all of his friends.

Tim Belk had received his master's degree in English from the University of South Carolina and come to live on Port Republic Street and teach at USCB. He became famous as a gifted and hard-nosed teacher of the language, a stickler for grammar who considered a dangling participle a minor crime against humanity. He was passionate about literature, music, and all the arts, and he was the kind of Southerner I had only encountered in literature. He seemed to drift out of the pages of Carson McCullers and would have looked natural with a walk-on part in a Tennessee Williams play. It was true. I had met no one remotely like him at The Citadel. At that first meeting, Tim

Belk and I had no idea he would one day have leading roles in the novels I would write. He would make
his original appearance as himself, playing the piano
for my Daufuskie students in *The Water Is Wide*. In
The Lords of Discipline, he took the stage as Tradd
St. Croix, a Charleston aristocrat who was part of a
quartet of roommates bound by the infinite resources
of their deep affection for each other. When *South of
Broad* came out, I granted Tim one of the most pivotal
roles in the book as Trevor Poe, a gay piano player
in San Francisco. Note that gayness has become a
theme here.

I consider the two years in Beaufort when I taught
high school as perhaps the happiest time of my life.
My attraction to melodrama and suffering had not
yet overwhelmed me, but signs of it were surfacing.
No one had warned me that a teacher could fall so
completely in love with his students that graduation
seemed like the death of a small civilization. It was
that same year that I became best friends with Bernie
Schein, Mike Jones, George Garbade, and the inimitable Tim Belk.

Tim seemed sophisticated and worldly in a way
that made me feel as uncultured as a listless pearl. I
would sit on his porch after teaching and he would fix

me a martini in a real martini glass. He served wine that was not Ripple or Blue Nun. He served canapés that I thought were coverings for boats and had no idea were wonderful predinner snacks to be served on good china with cloth napkins. In those two years, Tim would introduce me to *The New Yorker, The New Republic, The Nation,* the short stories of Flannery O'Connor, the novels of Walker Percy, the poetry of James Dickey, and all the great classical music of the Western canon. He played the piano with an almost supernatural ease, and he never forgot a song or piece of music he'd heard. He was one of the most civilized men I've ever known and one of the funniest. Our friendship lasted almost fifty years and much of it was spent laughing.

The world was afire in the late sixties. The Tet Offensive and the murders of Martin Luther King and Bobby Kennedy occurred in 1968, and integration was still in its experimental stages at Beaufort High. It seemed to me I was living ten lifetimes that single year, and it was an exhilarating year to be curious and alive. That Tim Belk was gay was whispered about and talked about openly, intimated by some and taken for granted by others. Though my children don't believe me now and find it hilarious, I didn't know what being gay was. Though I had heard all the disparaging names from "queer" to "faggot," no one had ever told me that they actually were gay. At The Citadel, if you were caught in a homosexual embrace, you were beaten to a pulp and expelled from school that day. It was part of the school's harsh military code and there was no recourse to law. A gay Southerner was an abomination of the species; it was a verminous condition that could not be brought up in polite circles.

———

Tim Belk was closeted himself in those early Beaufort days, and dated some of the loveliest women in this town. I double-dated with him on many occasions. Later, he married a beautiful teacher from the academy once he'd packed his bags and lit out for his new life in San Francisco. Tim left several months before I was fired from my teaching job on Daufuskie Island, the year I learned that the "separate but equal" system of the American South was the biggest lie ever told by the part of the world I love the most. I lost teaching, I lost Beaufort, and I lost Tim Belk at the same time.

Before the dissolution of his marriage to Diane

("We divorced because of irreconcilable similarities"), the Ford Foundation rescued me, sending my family and me out to San Francisco. Tim got a job playing the piano at the Curtain Call in the theater district. My wife, Barbara, and Diane would go out on the town once a week, to dinner and the theater. Tim and I went out every Thursday night, and that is when he introduced me to his new life that he found glorious and far from shameful. One night after a show, Marlene Dietrich and Elaine Stritch came into the Curtain Call, and Tim heard Elaine ask the legendary Marlene if she would sing her World War II anthem "Lili Marlene." Instantly, Tim began playing the haunting theme and heard Marlene say to Elaine Stritch, "It is the wrong key." In the next movement of his fingers he had changed to her key and Marlene said, "The boy can play."

With Tim Belk's elegant accompaniment, Marlene Dietrich sang the song beloved by both Nazi and American soldiers on both sides of the trenches, and brought a screaming crowd roaring to its feet. Later, Tim and I would go barhopping through the city as we always did. The bars of San Francisco had a hundred faces and some were ornate and mysterious, others bizarre, but all welcoming when Tim and

I were young, our dream of what the world could be still fresh and quivering with life. At one bar, soon after the "Lili Marlene" night, Tim and I were arguing the merits of some new novel, when a fan of his from the Curtain Call tapped me on the shoulder and asked me to dance. This was not part of my own dream of the world. But it made me study my surroundings with greater awareness. I had often been in bars with only men when I was a cadet, and I had noticed that people were dancing to a band in a room separate from the bar. Before this definitive moment, I had not noticed that they were all men dancing with each other. Tim looked horrified, but I'd become friendly with the man who asked me to dance, and I was raised by a mother who taught her kids never to hurt anyone's feelings. I said I'd be glad to and I followed the young man to the dance floor. He was from South Carolina, Greer, I believe, and I said, "You want to teach these boys to shag?"

"Delighted," he said.

"Mind if I lead?" I asked, and he said he'd love it if I did.

We shagged and the kid had great moves. After the dance, I thanked my partner and returned to the bar and sat beside Tim.

"You got something to tell me, pal?" I said.

That night, we stayed up talking 'til dawn and Tim told me his real life story, the one that gay Southern men were not allowed to tell back then. He told me he had realized he was gay as a small boy growing up in Fort Mill, South Carolina, and how the knowledge filled him with terror and self-loathing. He described the soul-killing loneliness it entailed, the nightmare of not only being different, but being something despised, vermin-like, a monstrous creation cut off from both society and God.

When *The Lords of Discipline* was published in 1980, I came through San Francisco on a book tour and spent the weekend in Tim's mid-level flat in a classic Victorian home on Union Street. More than anyplace I've ever been, Tim's home shimmered with romance and good taste. It looked like a space where great poetry would seize hold of you and shake the language out of you. When we awoke, Tim and I would drink coffee and eat croissants in a hidden-away garden lush with rosebushes and green climbing vines. We would talk about Beaufort—always Beaufort—then we would walk down and have lunch at the Washington Square Bar & Grill, where I learned about the taste of Dungeness crab and Petrale sole and met some of the grand characters who composed the bohemian life of North Beach.

It was on that trip that I made a huge meal for fifteen of Tim's gay friends. I started cooking at five and the party didn't break up until two in the morning. Nothing has ever made me laugh as much as gay humor in its perversity, punning, repartee, and yes, its pure and delightful wickedness. Many of these guys told stories about their childhoods in small towns across America that were heartbreaking and screamingly funny in the retelling. It was like hearing the tales of a leper colony for boys marked forever by the shame of being born the way they were supposed to be. Fifteen years later, Tim showed me a photograph of all of us attending that party and everyone, except Tim and me, had died of AIDS. Tim was dying of it when he showed me the snapshot.

I'd been living with my family in Italy when I read a report in the *International Herald Tribune* about a mysterious disease that was killing gay men in San Francisco and New York. I ran to the telephone and dialed Tim Belk's number in San Francisco. When he answered in his refined, cultured Southern accent, I said, "Tim, whatever you are doing in your unspeakable gay life, I want you to stop this minute. No more hanky-panky for you, son."

"So you've heard rumors of the plague as far away as Rome," Tim answered. "Don't you worry. You're talking to Sister Timothy Immaculata at this very moment. I'm in the midst of a life of purity, chastity, and good works. I attract wolf whistles from the cutest boys whenever I go to the Castro district wearing my nun's habit. But I keep tripping over these damn rosary beads."

"No jokes, Tim," I said. "This scares the living hell out of me."

"It scares you?" Tim said. "I'm so scared by this, I'm thinking of going back to the dark side. I'm thinking about dating women again."

"I'm not suggesting anything that drastic or repulsive to your deviant nature," I said.

"Pat, you know I've always thought you were gay," Tim teased.

"You told me I wasn't good-looking enough to be gay," I said.

Tim said, "Sadly, you're right. I think your dilemma's incurable."

As we were speaking that day, Tim had already

contracted the virus and the whole nature of our friendship was about to change. Because of the AIDS epidemic, I know of few American families who were not affected either indirectly or profoundly by the spread of the virus. It tore through the San Francisco area like some biblical plague that rolled across the city with that unearthly fog that stole up the Bay each afternoon. Only two of Tim Belk's large circle of gay friends did not die from the disease. It cast a hangman's pall over the entire city and caused unbearable grief in the households that had raised those boys across the American landscape. Over and over again, I encountered friends of Tim's whose families had renounced them forever when they found out their son or daughter was homosexual. These announcements not only infuriated these parents, but repulsed them to such a degree their sons and daughters arrived in San Francisco abandoned, without any bonds of family to support them. As a result, the gay men I met succeeded in forming themselves into an articulate tribe that was both rowdy and indivisible. San Francisco had freed them to be what they were born to be; AIDS made them political and the whole nation changed in its wake.

Tim Belk's flat on Union Street turned into a visitors' center for all of Tim's South Carolina friends. A generous host, he entertained a traveling circus of his Beaufort friends, and over a hundred of us stayed in his light-filled guest room on an alley that dipped down into the heart of North Beach. He gave a tour of the city that lasted for hours as he drove his car from Potrero Heights through Haight-Ashbury, to the mansions of Pacific Heights, the carnival-like atmosphere of the Castro, to the alleyways of Nob Hill. People would stay a week at a time and sometimes longer. With the city laid out like a white chessboard below him and the blue gleaming Bay in the distance with its regattas, and ship traffic at the Marin Headlands in the distance, he would declare in a prayer-like voice that San Francisco was the most beautiful city in the world. Then, in a tribute to all of our shared past, he would admit that Beaufort was just as lovely in its own lush, indefinable way. Each year he returned to Beaufort and brought great joy with his visits, parties galore, and his singular gift for finding magic in every piano that came his way.

After he was diagnosed as HIV positive, Tim and I used to talk at least once a week. As always, we talked literature, politics, and music, and he would tell me about the famous clubs and restaurants he had played in, from the top of the Mark Hopkins to Ernie's and notable gay bars the length and breadth of the city. He also became famous for playing at parties for high society in San Francisco, and over the years brought his skills into the peerless mansions of the Gettys and the Aliotos, and would always draw a crowd with his compendious knowledge of song and the virtuosity he brought to requests for Chopin, Schubert, and Mozart. All this was done as Tim sat there in his tuxedo with his bourbon and lit cigarette, and he kept up a charming line of social patter that had the entire room singing with him at the end of the evening. He made the whole American South look good in every room he entered, and his Southernness and handsomeness were all part of the package.

In 1988, Tim visited me in Atlanta and I saw for the first time the price that AIDS had begun to exert on his body. He came to my house having lost over twenty pounds since I'd last seen him, and his face covered with sores I'd once seen on several of his friends.

"My God, Tim," I gasped. "What's wrong?"

"Come hug the Elephant Man," he said, and I did.

"Don't worry, they can cure this. But soon, I'll come down with something they can't cure," he said.

"I think all this happened because I made out with some trashy girl in high school."

"You wish," I said.

The next year, my wife, Lenore, and I bought a house on Presidio Drive in San Francisco. Tim had not seemed afraid of dying, but very afraid of how he would die. His family was small and he feared being crippled or demented or incontinent. I heard it as a fear of dying alone. So my family and I moved to San Francisco, and I moved there with the purpose of helping Tim Belk die. In the four years I lived in his city, Tim and I became best friends as the relentlessness of his disease began to exert its undermining power over him.

Each day we spoke by telephone, and several times a week I would visit him on Union Street. On Sundays, we always had lunch at the Washington Square Bar & Grill, and we sat at a place of honor by the window so we could observe the human traffic spilling into the park with its kites and Frisbee-catching dogs. A community developed around us, and Leslie was our sharp-tongued waitress and Michael poured our Bloody Marys and a whole civilization came and went as we sat and talked about the state of the world as fifty Sundays went by and Tim lost more weight.

The movie version of *The Prince of Tides* came out in 1991 and I escorted Tim to every party I could, and he was paid good money to play at several of them. He enjoyed the hoopla of the events far more than I did, but I'd fallen in love with movies when Tim Belk hosted a movie series at the Breeze Theatre back in Beaufort. At the premiere, Tim sat beside me and murmured with pleasure at the sumptuous music that opened the movie, and the stunning shots of the town where we had first met twenty-five years before.

Soon after that premiere, one of Tim's friends dropped by when we were having lunch and said, "There's a gay kid from South Carolina who's dying of AIDS. His family won't have anything to do with him and his friends don't know where he is. They're frantic to find him."

"Hey Tim," I said, after his friend left. "I'll be damned if I'm gonna let some kid from South Carolina die of AIDS alone."

"I've been thinking the same thing," Tim answered. "Let's find him."

So Tim Belk and I began to search a part of San Francisco we knew nothing about. I described this in *South of Broad*, when a gay man named Trevor Poe disappears from sight in San Francisco and straight friends go looking for him to bring him back to Charleston. Trevor Poe, of course, was the fictional counterpart of Tim Belk. Tim and I delivered lunch and dinner to dying men who were staying at last-stand hotels in the Tenderloin, a god-awful place on few tourist maps. We would bring meals to men who would be dead within the week or month. We made phone calls to their families, gave them money, bought them groceries. I always asked them if they had met any young man from South Carolina. After weeks of searching, we found the man in a hospital less than four blocks from my house. His name was Jay Truluck and he was from the town of Turbeville, South Carolina.

Tim and I found him in a garden, sitting in a wheel-chair, completely blind. He was twenty years old.

"It could be worse, Jay," I said. "You could be in Turbeville, South Carolina."

Jay Truluck almost fell out of his wheelchair laughing.

"I'm from Fort Mill," Tim said. "It couldn't be that small."

"Trust me," Jay said. "It is."

So we became good friends with Jay Truluck and his suite mate, Jimmy Love, and Jimmy's exquisite mother and the golden-limbed Charlie Gallie, who was taking great care of both young men and dozens of other stricken patients around the city. Charlie became one of our best friends from that day onward. Those years were terrible, but a strange aura of charity and goodness came together during that time of epidemic. All of us were having dinner at my house on Presidio when Mrs. Love received a phone call that both Jimmy and Jay had died, just minutes apart. Tim and I met Jay Truluck's mother and sister at the airport and drove them to the funeral home for the final viewing.

In a country Southern accent, Mrs. Truluck said to me as I led her by the arm up to her son's casket, "Wasn't my Jay a beautiful boy?"

"Brace yourself, Mrs. Truluck," I warned. "He's not beautiful anymore."

When she saw her son's AIDS-ravaged face, she collapsed into my arms. Tim and I left her and Jay's devastated sister weeping openly over his casket as we retreated to the rear of the chapel.

Tim was furious and said, "I'd like to slap the hell out of both of them. They should've been here with Jay."

"Tim, they're Southern just like you and me. They

were just being true to how they were raised. Surely, we can understand that," I said.

"I hate when you go all sentimental and Christian on me," Tim said. "That's exactly what's wrong with your writing."

Tim never liked anything I wrote. As an English teacher, he insisted the prose be spare, unadorned, unflashy, but hard-hitting and severe. From the beginning of my career in Beaufort, Tim found my writing overcaffeinated, pretentious, and blowsy.

"Have you never heard of the eloquence of simplicity, Pat?" Tim Belk would say.

I would answer, "I'm after something else, Belk. The elegance of grotesque overwriting and egregious excess."

"But you're making me a character in all your overblown novels," Tim said. "I'm a man of Shakespearean depth, but I get a hack like you to tell my story."

"Therein lies your tragedy, Belk," I would say.

"You'd be a much better writer had you only been born gay," Tim said.

"Therein lies my tragedy." We could always make each other laugh.

In 1996, Tim began to die in earnest. On my book

tour for *Beach Music* we met at the Washington Square Bar & Grill and openly discussed his death for the first time. He now weighed less than a hundred pounds and had assumed that haunted, skeletal look of all AIDS patients at the very end. He held my hand as we talked, and his grip was shaky. A resignation to the inevitable had entered his voice, when I had an idea.

"Let's go on a final trip, Tim. It's on me and we'll go first class all the way. Doubleday is sending me to England and Ireland soon, and we can have one last legendary good time together."

"My bags are packed," Tim Belk said and that next spring, over the Atlantic, Tim and I toasted our years of friendship with a bottle of champagne. By then we had taken many trips together and found ourselves companionable in travel. Now, we promised to have the time of our lives and make this trip famous among all our friends. When we got off in Heathrow, there was an announcement on the loudspeaker for Tim to report to the Delta message center. Tim's doctor from San Francisco ordered Tim to report to a London hospital and Tim became one of the first human beings on earth to be put on the "cocktail," the intricate series of drugs that stopped the epidemic

in its tracks. To us, that trip took on mythic propor-
tion. We had our finest time together as friends on
this earth. Tim always referred to it as the trip that
saved his life.

Tim Belk did not die of AIDS. On October 21,
2014, I received the news of Tim Belk's death when
I was speaking at the Southern Festival of Books in
Nashville. He had gone into toxic shock after a kid-
ney infection and died in the hospital. His friends
mourned him all over the world. But our tears min-
gled with bursts of laughter and an affection that
was borderless and somehow sublime. He changed
my whole life and the way I saw the whole world. I
was lucky to know him, to love him, and to be trans-
formed by his love of me. I did not cry until I spoke
with Laura and Matthew Ringard, the friends he
had met through me only three years before. They
were devastated, and through their loss I felt myself
collapse. As I rode through the bomb plant between
Aiken and Allendale, I fell apart.

His light has gone out, but the music plays on.

Great love . . .

The Best Night in the Life of This
Aging Citadel Point Guard . . .

||||||||||||||

JANUARY 2015

I'll not pretend this is not one of the greatest nights of my life and one of the most surprising. In the history of American letters, no writer has had such a troublesome and controversial relationship with his college. I'm personally responsible for much of that tension and I'm fully aware of that. But, when I was a cadet at The Citadel, I decided I was going to try to become an American writer and I found myself encouraged to do this by my English professors Doyle, Carpenter, and Harrison, with a generous push from the history department of Conger, Martin, and Addington. I took every course taught by the magisterial Oliver Bowman, who let me in on the secrets of human psychology. Though I often lamented not going to an Ivy League college, I've talked to many of my contemporaries who did. They talk of great parties, drunkenness, and the great pleasure of midnight conversation and easy sex. I survived the toughest plebe system on earth, was taught by professors who cherished and loved me, and I was at my desk during Evening Study Period for four straight years. Now I think I had the best preparation to write novels of any writer of my time. I brought some of The Citadel's fighting spirit into my life of words with me. From the beginning, I've told journalists that I planned to write better than any writer of my era who graduated from an Ivy League college. It sounds boastful and it is. But The Citadel taught me that I was a man of courage when I survived that merciless crucible of a four-year test that is the measure of The Citadel experience. I'm the kind of writer I am because of The Citadel.

Though I was not welcome on this campus for thirty years, my name will now be on a plaque hanging in McAlister Field House in perpetuity. It will hang there because I am a writer. But to me, it will be there because once I was young and raring to go and could bring a basketball up court and do it fast. Once

I was a Citadel basketball player with the name of my college spelled out on my jersey and I think the happiest boy that ever lived on earth.

In 2002, I published a book called *My Losing Season* after I saw the brilliant shooting guard John DeBrosse in a bookshop outside of Dayton, Ohio. That day we talked about our 1966–67 team long into the night, and I realized that year still carried all the agonies and splendors of sport in a single tormented season. I started to write that book, and visited all the teammates I had abandoned after we lost a heartbreaking game in overtime to Richmond in the Southern Conference tournament.

I had fallen in love with my teammates that year and never had the human decency to let them in on the secret. By going back to find the heart of my basketball team, I found my way back to the soul of my college. My teammates, in the grandeur and despair of their memories, provided the means for me to explore the regions of myself that led to the fierce pride I take in being a Citadel man. In *The Lords of Discipline*, I tell of my disgust with the plebe system, but that is not a complete truth; it was the savage abuse of the system that I loathed. It was the cruelty to boys under the guise of leadership that I rejected from the first day I walked into Padgett-Thomas Barracks until the last. I never raised my voice to a plebe. I was raised in the Marine Corps and I was taught as a boy that you feed your own men before you feed yourself. It was my belief then, and it remains so today, that my platoon who loves and respects me will slaughter your platoon that hates you. But here is the great lesson I took from the plebe system—it let me know exactly the kind of man I wanted to become. It made me ache to be a contributing citizen in whatever society I found myself in, to live out a life I could be proud of, and always to measure up to what I took to be the highest ideals of a Citadel man—or, now, a Citadel woman. The standards were clear to me and they were high, and I took my marching orders from my college to take my hard-won education and go out to try to make the whole world a better place.

The Citadel gave me all of this and then gave me one of the greatest gifts of my life—it allowed me to be a college basketball player, to represent my college from the hills of West Virginia to the banks of the Mississippi to the night lights of New Orleans. I tested myself against great players from Florida State, Auburn, Virginia Tech, Clemson, George Washington, and thirty other teams around the South. Those great players taught me agonizing lessons about myself and my limits as an athlete. They taught me I was not very good, but I learned the same lessons every day from my splendid teammates at practice. I was a mediocre player out of his league in a very tough Southern Conference. But Lord have mercy on my soul, I loved that game with a passion that remains with me to this glorious night.

Let me tell you how it was. My guys and I would dress for the game and listen to the field house filling up with the noise of a fired-up crowd. Let's play Davidson, the year they were ranked number one in the nation at the beginning of the year. I want the place packed to the rafters and I want the whole Corps there. When you're a jock at The Citadel, you play for the Corps and there is nothing on earth to compare to the thunder and excitement and raw menace of the Corps screaming for their team. The Citadel band goes wild when you take to the court for the outcry of the Corps, and it is that superb band that provides the musical score with its theme of wildness, and oneness, as the Corps rises in unison, its huge demon-driven voice urging its team on. Under the boards, Dan Mohr grabs a rebound, tosses it to John DeBrosse, who hits one on the wing and I take it flying down the court—yes—and I said "flying" and I once felt like a winged, unstoppable creature when I led my team on a fast breakout that polished the floor with my golden teammates filling the lanes around me and I heard Hooper or Connor calling from the left— Bridges filling the right lane and the opposing team sprinting to cut off our mad dash to the basket. This scene played out in eighty games over my career as a Citadel point guard and I would go flashy and show-offy when I neared to top of the key and watched the eyes of the guard who was supposed to stop me. I turned my head to the left or to the right and if I saw him overplaying I would streak past him, just because I could and I wanted to put on a show for the Corps and my teammates. If the big man came up too fast to stop me, I'd lay the ball off to Tee Hooper or Doug Bridges and they would fly through the air to score. The Corps would ignite and explode in a pandemo-nium of roaring and chanting, and they put a primal fear into the hearts of the enemy who dared get in our way. Eighty nights of my life on earth were spent with the name of The Citadel emblazoned across my chest. I had never been so deeply alive before, and so rarely have since.

But it was my team, my team, my bruised and

damaged team, that was my greatest gift from that year—Dan Mohr, Jimmy Halpin, John DeBrosse, Dave Bornhorst, Bob Cauthen, Doug Bridges, Tee Hooper, Bill Zycinsky, Greg Connor, Al Kroboth, Brian Kennedy. I grow weak when I think about these guys, the way it felt to be around them, to be part of them. Our coach was the Ahab-like Mel Thompson and we fought through that year with his heel on our throats. He was a man of relentless fierceness and he ran us as a gulag rather than a team. Several of us would vomit from exhaustion after practice, and those practices were more physically exhausting than anything we ever suffered during the plebe system. Ten out of those twelve players had a moment in their career where they scored over twenty points in a Citadel varsity game, and the whole team averaged over eighty points a game before the era of the three-point shot. That team could play ball, but I believe it got its heart cut out by a coach who didn't know what he had. They were magical young men who have lived exemplary lives as Citadel men. All twelve of us graduated, many with gold stars and most with time on the dean's list. They have also become one of the most famous college basketball teams in history. When *My Losing Season* came out, I got letters from some of the most famous coaches in the country, coaches of all sports. Professional basketball players wrote me, the book was featured at the ACC championship tournament. It was used as a halftime special during the NBA championship. Whenever I sign new books, people ask me questions. "How's Root doing? Is DeBrosse still coaching? Did Connor ever get a date? What happened to Zipper? Did Bridges ever apologize to you for getting you kicked off the team? Is Barney still a nut?"

The book is being taught in high schools and colleges around the country. Young men and women have applied to The Citadel after reading this book. My team is going to live on in some library forever. I finally got to tell my team how I felt about them, and I finally got to tell my college how I felt about The Citadel.

So I've lived a lucky life and this night is the wonderful conclusion of a very long war between my college and myself. I speak to you in a room that is named for The Boo, and his portrait is watching from behind me. My name will hang among the greatest athletes ever to play for the long gray line, and I could not carry the jock of a single one of them. I chose to go into this hall of fame as a Green Weenie, what Dave

Bornhorst called the second string of the Citadel basketball team, and it was the Green Weenies who kept the spirit of sport and competition alive for me. Their fire and their loyalty and their steadfastness moved me, and I claim myself as one of them tonight. I want every second-stringer in the history of this school to know that a Green Weenie is going up on the Wall. I began this journey in 1963 and it reaches some beautiful and surprising conclusion by the generosity of this committee tonight.

But, ladies and gentlemen, I told you a long time ago why this night means everything to me.

I'm the guy who wrote his first line in *The Lords of Discipline* for all the world to hear. It summed up the way I felt about The Citadel and always have—

I wrote four words. "I wear the ring."

I thank you with all my heart for this priceless honor.

The Summer I Met My First
Great Man

||||||||||||

JANUARY 19, 2015

In the summer of 1961, when I was a fifteen-year-old boy, I was lucky to have the great Bill Dufford walk into my life. I had spent my whole childhood taught by nuns and priests, and there was nothing priestly about the passionate, articulate man William E. Dufford who met me in the front office of Beaufort High School dressed in a sport shirt, khaki pants, and comfortable shoes in a year that history was about to explode in the world of South Carolina education circles. Because he did not wear a white collar or carry a long rosary on his habit, I had no idea that I was meeting the principal of my new high school. In my mind I thought, as I saw him moving with ease and confidence in the principal's main office that day, that he must be a head janitor in the relaxed, un-Catholic atmosphere of my first day at an American public school. It was also my first encounter with a great man.

I was a watchful boy being raised by a father I didn't admire. In a desperate way, I needed the guidance of someone who could show me another way of becoming a man. It was sometime during that year when I decided I would become the kind of man that Bill Dufford was born to be. I wanted to be the type of man that a whole town could respect and honor and fall in love with—the way Beaufort did when Bill Dufford came to town to teach and shape and turn its children into the best citizens they could be.

Bill gave me a job as a groundskeeper at Beaufort High School that summer between my junior and senior years of high school. He had me moving wheelbarrows full of dirt from one end of campus to another. He had me plant grass, shrubs, trees, and he looked at every patch of bare earth as a personal insult to his part of the planet. At lunch, he took me to Harry's Restaurant every day and I watched him as he greeted the movers and shakers of that beautiful town beside the Beaufort River. He taught me, by example, how a leader conducts himself, how the principal of a high school conducts himself, as he made his way from table to table, calling everyone by their first names. He made friendliness an art form. He represented the highest ideals of what I thought a Southern gentleman could be. He accepted the great regard of his fellow townsmen as though that were part of his job description. That summer, I decided to try to turn myself into a man exactly like Bill Dufford. He made me want to be a teacher, convinced me that there was no higher calling on earth, and none with richer rewards, and none more valuable in the making of a society I would be proud to be a part of. I wanted the people of Beaufort, or any town I lived in, to light up when they saw me coming down the street. I was one of a thousand kids who came under the influence of our magnificent principal Bill Dufford. For him, we all tried to make the world a finer and kinder place to be.

Bill Dufford was raised in Newberry in the apartheid South, where the civil rights movement was but a whisper gathering into the storm that would break over the South with all of its righteousness and power. Though Bill had been brought up in a segregated society, he charged to embrace the coming of freedom to Southern black men and women with a passionate intensity that strikes a note of awe and wonder in me today. He went south to the University of Florida the year I graduated from high school, and came under the influence of some of the greatest educational theorists of his time. He returned to South Carolina with a fiery commitment to the integration movement in his native state. No other white voice spoke with his singular power. He headed up the school desegregation department, which sent people into all the counties in the state to help with the great social change of his time. I know of no white Southerner who spoke with his eloquence about the great necessity for the peaceful integration of the schools in this state. What I had called greatness when I first saw him in high school had transfigured itself into a courage that knew no backing down, a heroism that defied the ironclad social laws of his own privileged station, being from a great Newberry family.

Today, we honor Bill Dufford for a life well lived. In recent years, he has been an articulate spokesman for the diversity issue in our society. Because of Bill, his family donated their magnificent house to serve as Newberry College's alumni house. The Dufford family has made large contributions to the Newberry Opera House, one of America's loveliest buildings. Hundreds of his students went into teaching and education because of him. Today you honor Bill Dufford, one of the finest men I've ever met. It does not surprise me that you are honoring him; it just surprises me it took so long.

Remember, I was fifteen years old when I thought I had met my first great man. Mr. Dufford, it is a remarkable honor to introduce you today.

Andie MacDowell at the
Beaufort Film Festival

FEBRUARY 14, 2015

In Beaufort tonight, we gather together to praise the career of Andie MacDowell, the extraordinarily beautiful and accomplished actress who has dazzled the world since her appearance in *Greystoke: The Legend of Tarzan, Lord of the Apes*. It was the only time in my life that I've ever been jealous of Tarzan. Though I knew he'd always be stronger than me, I always thought I'd be a lot smarter. But anyone smart enough to fall in love with Andie MacDowell seemed a lot brighter than I would ever be. At this film festival and on this night, we are here to praise all the bright magic that has entered into our lives from the fantastical world of film. When I was a small boy, I realized that I was falling in love with every actress who appeared on-screen. My own mother told me that she would leave my father and her seven children the moment she heard Clark Gable tapping on her bedroom window. My own beloved wife, Cassandra King, admits, while holding a Bible, that if Brad Pitt ever calls, I can give all her clothes to Goodwill, but she'll be taking her Victoria's Secrets with her.

It is beauty and story and the high realms of imagination that make us prisoners to Hollywood. We find ourselves more alive, more susceptible to dreaming, when a theater goes dark and that unutterably thrilling moment begins when we wait with held breath to laugh, to weep, to understand, to have our lives changed forever. It was not just the Greeks who needed gods and goddesses—all human beings have needed them, since the dawn of mankind.

The goddess we honor tonight is Andie MacDowell, born in Gaffney, South Carolina, of all places. But we know anything's possible now. Beaufort has seen Candice Glover take our nation by storm. Joe Frazier was heavyweight champion of the world and once walked these streets. Tom Hanks played *Forrest Gump* while living in Beaufort. *The Big Chill* was

made here. We have come to know that South Carolina is a place where the most uncommon fantasies
come true. While dressing tonight, who among you
was not excited beyond your capacity to imagine just
setting your eyes on Andie MacDowell? Which of
you is cold enough not to be moved to speechlessness
by her ineffable beauty, by her otherworldly talent?
I went nuts over her performance in *Sex, Lies, and
Videotape* and wish I'd been an understudy in all the
Sex parts of that film. Who did not think that they
had seen one of the great movies of their time when
they walked out of *Groundhog Day?* Bill Murray had
the greatest life on-screen; each day he was doomed
to wake up again and relive his life with Andie Mac-
Dowell. Lord, Lord, give me such a life. I went with
two gay friends to *Four Weddings and a Funeral* and, as
they fell in love with Hugh Grant, I cast myself adrift
again onto those South Carolina tides that only
Andie could make for me. Her film *Unstrung Heroes*
is a personal favorite of mine, and I'd like to tell you
I'm a much deeper man, tell you it's her talent that
gets me every time. Yes, her talent plays a great part,
but beauty is a gift from God and I am simply one of
God's simple creatures, who falls in love with Andie
every time I see one of her films.

Andie MacDowell, as I present this well-deserved award to you, let me present you to the town of Beaufort. From vast experience, I know how much this town can love. Please accept this award that comes from the heart of this town I love best in the world. The great actress Andie MacDowell, please allow my town to make you feel as loved as you deserve to be.

Mina & Conroy Fitness Studio

||||||||||||||||

MARCH 21, 2015

Hey, out there,
I've just opened a place of business in downtown Port Royal, South Carolina. It is an odd thing to be doing at my age. There is nothing on my résumé that indicates I'll be successful in this unusual endeavor. But I'm doing it because there are four or five books I'd like to write before I meet with Jesus of Nazareth—as my mother promised me—on the day of my untimely death, or reconcile myself to a long stretch of nothingness as my nonbelieving friends insist.

Three years ago I nearly died from my own bad

habits. At my lowest point I made an awkward vow to myself that if I could survive the crisis, I would try to improve my complete lack of dedication to my own health. I stopped drinking at that moment, told my splendid doctor Lucius Laffitte that I was going to do what he told me. I hired my next-door neighbor, the fetching Liz Sherbert, to be my nutritionist, and for two years I've tried to satisfy my great interior hunger with a diet that would satisfy a full-grown squirrel but has done little to conquer the hippopotamus that lives within me. Still, I lost a quick twenty pounds and have learned to put up with Liz's surprise commando raids on my household to check on forbidden foods she finds in my refrigerator. When she spies me grazing on my front lawn, she shouts encouragement from her deck, "Greenery. Salads. That's the way to weight loss, Pat." Liz has encouraged me to shun all the foods I love and eat plentiful amounts of the things I despise. My lesson from this is never to hire a nutritionist who lives next door.

Dr. Laffitte also ordered me to exercise. In my youth I walked around disguised as an athlete, especially to myself. When I quit playing basketball at the age of forty, my weight increased every year until I turned into a Southern fat boy, to my utter horror.

Over the years, I hired personal trainers to abuse and shape up the fatted calf I'd become. From Europe to San Francisco, I hired a series of good men who were skilled practitioners of their art. But after a year or so I grew bored, and then had a back operation that affected my mobility for a long time. In 1996, I was diagnosed with type 2 diabetes, which I call "The Fat Boy's Disease." The doctors are too kind and diplomatic to call it that, but I believe it's an accurate description in my case.

I joined the Beaufort YMCA a few years ago. It's a terrific place founded by the actor Tom Berenger and his ex-wife, who is a well-known Beaufort beauty. Three times a week I would meet a friend, the novelist John Warley, at the Y and we would exercise together. While exercising, I noticed a young Okinawan woman working with her clients, and had never seen a physical therapist work with such dedication and compassion. With all her clients, including some who were elderly and some in wheelchairs, she gave her full attention and never looked around when someone was in her care. I hired Mina Truong as my personal trainer and went to see her twice a week. She was both a wonder and a stern taskmaster, so I started to feel muscles in places I'd forgotten I had them. Then, on a book tour, I hurt my back getting out of a car and did not see Mina for an entire year. It was at the end of that year that I nearly died in a Charleston hospital.

When I recovered from my illness, I signed up with Mina at the Y again. At first I went once a week, then three times, and then five times. I had marvelous fun with her, even though I could barely walk to the car after she had finished with me. But I started feeling better—much better than I had in years. Her skills in English are limited, and she'd apologize almost every time I saw her.

"So sorry, Mr. Pat. English very bad," she'd say.

"No problem, Mina. My Japanese is much worse."

"No, no, Mr. Pat. My English should be better," she'd say.

"Could you stop calling me Mr. Pat? It's driving me nuts. I feel like Marlon Brando in *The Teahouse of the August Moon.*"

"No, I must call you Mr. Pat. Out of respect. When you come to me, I did not know you. I not know you are very great man. A writer."

"Give me a break, Mina. I write pornography."

"What is this word? My English not good, Mr. Pat."

"I write dirty books. Naked men and women doing unspeakable things to each other."

"What is this unspeakable?" she said.

"You're not supposed to say it out loud."

"Dirty books? Bad books?"

"Yes, that's what I write. Now hurt me some more. Our time is not up."

"Mr. Pat, I never hurt you."

"You hurt me every time I see you," I said.

"No, I help you. I make you strong."

So, without my quite knowing it, I became Mina's unpaid English teacher over the past year, making certain that I brought in a few new words for her to learn each day. Because I lived in Italy for three years and never came close to grasping the language, I know that humor in a foreign tongue is a difficult, if not impossible, thing to master. If a single Italian ever told me a joke, I can assure you I didn't get it. At some point, I realized that poor Mina often had no idea I was kidding her. I know better than anyone that a Conroy sense of humor is not everyone's cup of green tea.

In the middle of doing leg lifts, Mina would ask me, "How do you feel, Mr. Pat?"

"I feel terrible," I'd say, gasping.

"Terrible. That is bad to feel? Terrible?"

"It's awful to feel terrible," I said.

"How can I make you feel better, Mr. Pat?"

"Call 9-1-1."

"Why 9-1-1, Mr. Pat?"

"I need an ambulance."

"Why you need this ambulance?"

"Because I'm dying. You're killing me, Mina."

"No, Mr. Pat. I help you."

"Tell the crew I need a wheelchair."

"Crew?"

"The men and women in the ambulance. They need a wheelchair because I can't walk."

"Why can't you walk, Mr. Pat?"

"Because you hurt me."

"Ah! It's a joke. I hear you are a funny man, Mr. Pat. How you feel?"

"Terrible."

Each week I could feel my body changing, hardening, growing stronger. Finally, I came to the wonderful conclusion that I was feeling much better than I had for years. My friends and family and long-suffering wife all told me I was looking better, but to be truthful, I still look like a linebacker who has gone painfully to seed. But I give all credit to Mina Truong, who has inspired me to work harder than I ever have before.

This past January, my beloved brother Mike went into surgery for a quadruple bypass that terrified the entire Conroy family, because Mike is the only one of us who knows how to get things done. He's the anchor to our whole family, so I can't imagine how complicated life would be if he was not around. But Mike is also tough as a walnut, and he came through the operation and never complained to a single person about the pain he endured. The operation was a complete success and Mike came home several days before his release date. I was as joyous as I was relieved when I went to the Y and sweet Mina was there with a worried look in her eyes.

"How is your brother, Mike, Mr. Pat?"

"Mike . . ." I said (and this next part of my personality is irritating and inexplicable even to me, but it is my personality and this is how I answered poor Mina of Okinawa): "The operation didn't go very well, Mina."

"What do you mean, Mr. Pat?" she asked.

"Mike's dead. But we can't let that interfere with my workout."

"Your brother? He is dead? You must be very sad, Mr. Pat. You must go to his wife. To comfort her."

"Naw, I never liked her much."

"When is brother Mike's funeral?"

"It's going on right now, Mina. I knew I couldn't miss my workout. And there's a sale on tulip bulbs at Lowe's," I said, and by the look on Mina's face I knew I would have some trouble bringing this subject to a close.

Mina helped me by starting to cry. Large, heartfelt tears fell from her eyes as she wept at the death of my unmourned brother. I tried to figure out a graceful means of exit from a joke that offered few avenues of escape.

Finally, I said, "Mina, I forgot. I got a call on my cell phone before I got to the Y. Mike didn't die. They made a mistake."

"Mistake?" she asked in tears.

"Yeah, they got him confused with the guy in the next room. He looked a lot like Mike. But my brother's fine."

"You told me lie. About your brother's death, Mr. Pat," Mina said.

"It was a joke. But it must not translate well into Japanese," I said.

"Joke? You make joke about your poor brother. He die. That is a terrible, terrible joke, Mr. Pat."

"Yeah, it is awful, Mina. I apologize," I said.

"You are a very, very bad man, Mr. Pat."

"Yes, I knew you would find that out one day. Now hurt me," I said.

Mina then put me through the toughest regimen of exercise His Fatness had experienced in a long time. I knew that there was some kind of subliminal punishment involved, but I felt I deserved it. The next day when I walked into the Y, Mina said, "How is your poor brother, Mike, Mr. Pat?"

"Very bad, Mina. Mike died last night. I'm very sad."

Mina burst out laughing and a fellow employee at the Y walked by at the time and asked her what was so funny.

"I told her my brother died last night," I said.

"It is a lie. Nothing he says is true. No word is true. Ever," Mina said.

I said, "Mina, you've got a great sense of humor."

"No, Mr. Pat. You turn me into a terrible person. Today, we do aerobics. Fun, yes?"

"I hate aerobics," I said.

"It help you not be sad, Mr. Pat," Mina said. "Over poor Mike dying."

But there was trouble in paradise. The YMCA was one of the happiest places I've ever been in Beaufort. I fell in love with the women at the front desk and took great pleasure in getting to know various people who worked out at the same time I did. But one Friday, Mina told me she had been suspended for ten days. When I asked why, she told me she could not discuss it with me because of YMCA rules. I went down to discuss it with the director and he told me he could not talk about it because it was "a personnel issue." So I'd hit upon the bureaucratic world I despise and knew it was a lost battle even to enter that strange, octopus-armed territory. My friend Aaron Schein, who had also fallen in love with Mina, resigned from the Y in disgust.

Mina returned, but I could feel her tension every time she worked me out. Finally, two weeks ago, I asked Mina to lunch and she brought her two best friends, Lin Pope and her husband, Bruce. It seemed as though Mina was to be fired that Saturday. I suggested she resign, and she did so that very moment in the restaurant Moondoggies. Within seconds, not minutes, she received a reply: "Accepted."

"Now, Mina, what are you going to do?" I said. "I need you to keep me alive. So I'm real interested."

The following day, we rented a small office at 832 Paris Avenue in Port Royal, a town that includes Parris Island in its district. Ten days later we opened shop at Mina & Conroy Fitness Studio. I warned Mina that if my photograph ever appeared on any advertising, she would not have a single client.

"I'm not a good walking advertisement for a fitness studio," I explained. Mina & Conroy is small, intimate, and a perfect place for me to spend part of the day for the rest of my natural life. We are having an open house on April 3, from four to seven in the evening, and I'm inviting anyone who'd like to come to be Mina's and my guest. Cassandra King and I will be signing books, and I might invite some of my other writer pals to come as well. There will be wine and cheese and we'll try to have a ball. Mina calls it her "castle," and I like the sound of her voice when she says it. I'm trying to get my brother Mike to come down. Mina's dying to meet him.

Great love . . .

A Few Things I Wish I Had Told
Ann Patchett...

||||||||||||||||

JUNE 16, 2015

Hey, out there,

I first became aware of the immensely gifted writer Ann Patchett when she published her first novel with my old publisher Houghton Mifflin. It was an old Boston firm located in a classical brick office building that seemed indigenous to the Boston Common and Back Bay. Houghton Mifflin satisfied every dream I'd ever had as an American boy who grew up wanting to be a writer. It was a palace of Boston WASP and its masthead sang out with distinguished New England names. I thought I'd be a Houghton Mifflin boy forever.

But the world of publishing was about to undergo a sea change in the creative lifetime of all writers. I thought my first editor, Shannon Ravenel, would be my editor forever. But she moved to Saint Louis before my first book even came out. Then I believed that the lovely, stately Anne Barrett would direct my career, but Anne retired, then died. I was given the young, dazzling Jonathan Galassi and I thought I'd stumbled into the lifetime of the greatest editor of his generation, and I had. But Jonathan was New York–bound, and New York–destined, and the mighty Random House recruited Jonathan for its own impressive stable of editors. I would have gone to Random House with Jonathan, because I recognized his genius and wanted to be part of it always, but the editors of Random House, in their infinite wisdom and ineptitude, insulted Jonathan and me when I went to sign up for my new novel, *The Prince of Tides*. Both Jonathan and I wince when we recall that dispiriting day whenever we get together in New York. Houghton Mifflin assigned me a new editor, Nan Talese, and she and I have been partners in whatever crimes against literature I've created in the last thirty years. Nan became my destiny and I left Houghton Mifflin, heartbroken, to join her at Doubleday. I plan to be with Nan for the rest of my life.

But Houghton Mifflin is still a cry within my writing heart. It seemed so right for me, an instrument perfectly tuned to the writer I was hoping to become. The firm was literary, low-keyed, and calm in its aristocratic singularity. The editors pushed books on me by their new novelists and writers. It thrilled me to read the first and second books of brand-new voices on the American scene. My teacher James Dickey had published his first novel, *Deliverance*, with them two years before I'd arrived on the scene. Philip Roth had begun his career with Houghton, then had lit out for New York. But I read the first books of Don DeLillo and Paul Theroux and Sylvia Wilkinson and Madison Smartt Bell. Anne Sexton was publishing her incendiary poetry at that time, and the Houghton Mifflin backlist was a writers' field of wonder.

Over my time there, I took special pleasure in reading the first works by young novelists, those fearless navigators who slipped into that perilous world with something new to say. Like all publishing houses, Houghton Mifflin was male-dominated, possibly a tad misogynist, and women writers seemed poorly represented when I first arrived. But like all great publishing houses, Houghton was itself a mirror of American society, and the great surge of women writers was already on the march. Late in my time at Houghton Mifflin, two young women arrived on the scene who were the talk of the company—Susan Minot with a novel called *Monkeys,* and Ann Patchett with one called *The Patron Saint of Liars.* Both were talented, all agreed, but both were also drop-dead beautiful.

Physical attractiveness does not make frequent visitations to the writers' world. When I attended a party celebrating the writer Jennifer Egan's first novel, Gay Talese came up to me in the middle of the gathering and said, "This isn't a writers' party. These people are way too good-looking to be writers. Writers are ugly people. This group is way too gorgeous to call themselves writers."

The talented Jennifer Egan is also a beauty and her husband is in theater and they had attracted a comely group among their New York friends. But Gay had a point and a great eye for detail, which has made him one of the greatest nonfiction writers this country has ever produced. Generally, writers descend from a lesser tribe, and whatever claim to beauty we have shows up on the printed page far more often than it does in our mirrors. Even as I write these words I think of dozens of writers, both male and female, who make a mockery of this generalization. But comeliness among writers is rare enough to be noteworthy.

Though I'm no longer part of the Houghton Mifflin family, I still keep up with their new young writers and I always wish for them success as a publishing company. One of the sales reps sent me a reading copy of Ann Patchett's first novel, *The Patron Saint of Liars*, and from the beginning she seemed like the real thing to me. Her voice was clear and original and I marked her down as a writer to watch. I attended a writers' conference at the University of Mississippi sometime in the blur that was the nineties for me; I stood in line to get a copy of her second novel, *Taft*, signed by her. We introduced ourselves to each other and I found her to be one of the most attractive women I'd ever met. She looked like one of those women you wish you could've met and married as a young man. She was poised, self-contained, delightful, and I thought *Taft* was a fulfillment of the great promise she showed in *The Patron Saint of Liars*. I thought she was still shaking free of those invisible handcuffs and chains of bondage that the writing schools of America impose on their grads. She was a survivor of the

Iowa Writers' Workshop, where they train the rogue elephants and the big cats of the writing world. It's both a cutting-edge and thought-cutting matrix that has produced some great writers and an endless regiment of failed ones. It is a savage gathering of wolves on the middle plains of Iowa, and I can't think of a more honorable or deadly arena in which an American writer can test his or her talent in the vast meanness of the writing world. I applied for admission to the Iowa Writers' Workshop, was turned down, and still consider it one of the great blessings of my writing career. But it didn't lay a hand on the strength of Ann Patchett's talent. It always makes the great ones better and the bad ones better, too.

I've lived in exciting times and I'd have it no other way. I was born during the disgraceful Jim Crow years of the South and was lucky enough to be raised by a Southern mountain woman who found the entire South evil. She and I watched the Old South crumble into dust around us, and we took enormous satisfaction in its fall. On the heels of the civil rights movement, women's liberation came hurtling down the turnpike and opened up the writing world for women of all kinds. I followed closely the career of Anne Rivers Siddons, Josephine Humphreys, Donna Tartt,

Diane Ackerman, Toni Morrison, Andrea Barrett, Alice Walker, Mary Hood, Doris Betts, Annie Dillard, Janis Owens, Louise Erdrich, Patricia Hampl, and dozens of others who both amazed me and filled me with pleasure. Recently, I've begun reading the eye-popping works of Barbara Kingsolver and discovering her as one of the great gifts of my sixty-eighth year. Joyce Carol Oates has written for so long and so well that her achievement has to be measured in miles, not feet. There has been no one like her in American letters. I once took a streetcar to the top of Nob Hill to get Lee Smith to sign the bagful of her books I'd collected over the years. Cassandra King, the woman I married in 1998, has published five novels since I first met her at a writers' conference in Birmingham. Though women writers were still a rarity when I began my career, they now dominate at every level and American letters are richer for it.

But, for me, Ann Patchett went to the top of the class when she published *Bel Canto,* a book that knocked my socks off and did the same with the reading public, who were as hungry for such a book as I was. I read it on Pawleys Island, one of the magical places on the South Carolina coast, after Doug Marlette finished it and raved about it. Reading half the night, I completed the book the following day. When Doug and I went swimming in the surf that night, we talked of nothing else. When literature works there is nothing like it in the world. Few books I've ever read worked as well as this one. Ann Patchett did that wondrous, walking-on-water kind of thing—she created a whole world that contained grand opera, the revolutionary spirit always alive and close to the surface in Latin America, a siege, a story of Shakespearean grandeur, unbearable tension that built up with the turning of every page, a savage denouement, love stories haunted by the approach of death, an ending that dissatisfied some critics, but that satisfied something in me—her passionate and grateful reader. I had literature all over my hands and face when I finished that book. I thought then and I think now it's one of the best novels I ever read or ever hope to read in my life. High praise? Yes, but joyfully given.

During my book tour I went to Nashville, Tennessee, a city that Ann Patchett has succeeded in making her own. She and her husband are vital members of the city and he is a splendid man, a doctor and Sewanee man, who knew my best friend at Beaufort High School, Bruce Harper, when they attended college together. I visited Ann Patchett's independent bookstore that she opened with Karen Hayes, a former sales rep for Random House, and it is a gathering place for book lovers all over the South. The store, called Parnassus Books, is populated by bright young people who know the stock and can tell you all about their own favorite books published that season. Every independent bookstore in this country has a sacramental feel to it these days, of something that needs to be preserved at all costs. Ann herself cuts a heroic figure in the publishing world by stepping into the breach and putting her own money into the survival of this amazing store. I think the city of Nashville understands this—a city without an independent bookstore is not much of a city at all. It's too much like a river without a current.

Ann Patchett introduced me to a crowd in an auditorium, in one of the most beautifully restored public schools in the country. It's right in the middle of downtown and reminded me of Sacred Heart, where I went to kindergarten in downtown Atlanta. I thought I'd get a chance to rave about her novels and books, but Ann conducted the interview and kept me talking about the subject at hand. She was bright and as lively and lovely as I'd imagined her to be. It was like being interviewed by Anna Karenina. In my earliest fantasies of being a writer, I never dreamed of such a night happening—to be questioned by a great novelist about a book I'd written. That belonged to the realm of impossibility when I started out, and she brought her own deep intelligence to the task of what was on my mind when I wrote this memoir about my family. I wish nights like that could linger more freshly in the memory, that they weren't so fragile and slippery and impossible to nail down for study in one's leisure. But the really great nights pass through you like whispers or shadows. They shimmer, but don't adhere. I never got to rave to Ann Patchett about her work, and that's what I had come to Nashville to do. I had a ton of pleasurable things to tell Ann about *State of Wonder* and her new book of essays, but the time never seemed right. But I wanted her to know how essential her writing has been to my reading life. I can only hope that one day, she'll read this.

Great love . . .

Conroy at Seventy—
Happy Birthday to Me

||||||||||||

OCTOBER 22, 2015

Hey, out there,

I've always taken great pleasure in reading the biographies of other writers whose books have sustained and gladdened my heart. Yesterday, I finished *The Last Love Song,* a biography of Joan Didion by Tracy Daugherty. Whenever I encountered Ms. Didion's prose it turned me into a grinning fool because of its strange perfection and her ability to make me see things in ways I never imagined. I once went to dinner with Joan Didion and her husband, John Gregory Dunne, at Elaine's. We were guests of my editor, Nan Talese, and her husband,

Gay Talese. Elaine's was a watering hole for writers and celebrities, and it was proof of their inferior palates that they chose that troubled restaurant to stem their hunger. I found myself in the men's room with the huge actor Mr. T that night. When I looked over as I stood beside him peeing, I said, "Mine's bigger," and Mr. T screamed with laughter and I've loved Mr. T since that moment.

From her writing, I thought that Joan Didion would prove elliptical and mysterious, and so she did. A beautiful woman, she took me in with a mermaid's dark eyes, but they could turn into a cobra's with the slight rise of an eyebrow. My instinct is to gush when I meet a writer I revere, but long experience has taught me it's a dangerous thing to do. Greg did not warm to my presence and I felt him pulling back from me, an old gunfighter's instinct I've long encountered in male writers, and, more frequently now, in women. I was worried that by praising his wife I would somehow diminish him, even though I talked about two of his novels that I'd really liked. I was also aware that Gay Talese might well have been the finest writer at the table that night. So I listened and took it all in and found myself delighted with the account of Joan Didion's life that I bought the day it was published.

The biography was a crash course in what had made me fall in love with Joan Didion's style in the first place. It had always been a point of amazement to me that Ms. Didion could hide all essences of herself in the beauty of her immaculate sentences. Though I could never fall in love with her soul, I could always be captive to her style. She lacked the interior eye, but absorbed everything that took place in her sight and hearing. As I suspected, she offered Mr. Daugherty no help at all in the writing of his book about her life. He wrote a splendid book without her help, and it's my theory he wouldn't have learned that much about her if she had granted him full access. Some people are like that; so are some writers.

I'm not like that. I've spent my whole writing life trying to find out who I am, and I don't believe I've even come close. But that knowledge grants me insight and causes me no despair. The journey has defined me, inspired me, and forced me to write on. I've tried to read the biography of every writer who has kept me awake at night, thrilled me with their talent to make a world I didn't know existed, and taken me on a joyride into the land of fiction, which has provided some of the greatest pleasures I've ever had. Over the years, I've read hundreds of biographies and all of them told me something I needed to know and what to watch out for and the collisions I needed to avoid. They fed the writer in me, and all of them told me that the world was the only thing that counted, that what I produced and its quality was all that mattered. It was at the writing desk that I would be made or broken. In every biography of every writer, that was the secret to our kingdom of words. No other measurement counted for anything at all.

I have some reckoning and summation entering into my own life. Two biographers have entered my life and it's made me take notice of my own troubled, untidy passage through time. Katherine Clark, a novelist and writer from Birmingham, has recently completed an oral biography that she took from more than two hundred hours of interviews she recorded over the past several years. I lack all gifts of reticence or caution, and every time Katherine relates some outrageous or libelous quote from the book, I wince then swear I never said such a thing. "I have it on tape, Pat," she says, winning each argument. She has captured me uncensored and the whole thing makes me think of root canals and colonoscopies.

The next biographer teaches English and Women's

Studies at Southern Illinois University at Edwards-ville and her name is Catherine Seltzer. She just pub-lished a book with the University of South Carolina Press called *Understanding Pat Conroy.* Catherine has undertaken the cheerless task of writing a conven-tional biography about me, and because my ego has swollen into elephantine dimensions in my dotage, I agreed to do it with one undebatable provision. Under no terms would I agree to cooperate with Dr. Seltzer on an "authorized biography." Often writ-ers make such demands on their biographers out of a desire to control their stories and what is written about them, their friends, and their family. I wouldn't participate in an authorized biography for any reason, because I thought it would be a betrayal of everything I thought I stood for in life. I told Catherine that if she didn't include the unexpurgated memories of my friends and enemies, ex-wives and girlfriends, hostile critics and others who have reason to renounce my career and life as a complete failure, her book would be worthless. The stories of when I acted like an asshole need to have equal weight with those rare moments of decency when I was of some credit to my species. There was to be no interference with her conclusions from me or my heirs. Catherine Seltzer agreed to all that. I required her to tell the life story I wasn't aware I lived, or the one I was ashamed of living.

This was all preamble to bring me to the subject of this letter. Much to my surprise, I'll be turning seventy years old at the end of this month. When I was thirty I think I looked at people who were seventy as frail relics of time who had all seen ivory-billed woodpeckers and passenger pigeons in their childhoods. I remember going to Kitty Mancini's fiftieth birthday party in Alexandria, Virginia, given by her children, Mike, Patty, and Sharon Mahoney, my three best friends from my grade school days, and I thought as I kissed that kindest of women that it was a shame she would be dead so soon. The same children gave Kitty a party on her ninetieth birthday in Richmond last year.

But the subject of death is a frequent one among my friends these days. Terry Kay, the novelist, has announced his demise on a daily basis for the last twenty years. I've worried about my friend Anne Rivers Siddons's health for the last five years. My wife, Cassandra, is a member of the Hemlock Society and hides potions in her closet I'm not to ask about on pain of divorce court. My irreplaceable friend Doug

Marlette died in his fifties in a Mississippi car wreck. Jane Lefco, who took care of my finances, died of an embolism while still beautiful and young. My brother Tom killed himself at thirty-four. I lost eight classmates in the Vietnam War and four of them were boys I loved.

So this number has deep resonance, and I'm taking it more seriously than I ever thought I would. It strikes a biblical chord in me. The town of Beaufort is throwing me a birthday party.

There is a great central flaw in my character that I've gone out of my way to conceal. Though I find a perfect comfort zone in all forms of chaos, I've never shown a similar ease when I discover any intrusion of joy or, God forbid, happiness inviting me to a party at their house. In my own lifetime, I've found myself resolute in the face of terrible abuse, the suicide of family and friends, divorce courts, plebe systems, the death of my mother and father, betrayal by people I adored, breakdown, humiliation, and the list goes on and on. It seemed like the natural state of human affairs to me, but it gave me enough time and material to write the books I once dreamed as a boy of writing.

Discord has been my theme. It has agitated me that I find myself approaching my seventieth birthday and have discovered within myself a joy I'd never once felt any capacity for having. To write it down strikes a chord of sappiness in me. But in my career, if I discovered something rising out of me, I took it as a point of honor to write it down. I've found myself studying my past of late, and though there has been a theme of discordance and tragedy in my work and life, I've been a supremely lucky man. But a happy one? This is a river without markers or navigational charts for me.

The University of South Carolina is throwing a party for me. They are calling it, I say with a seventy-year-old sigh, "Pat Conroy at 70." I know why I agreed to do it. It was a victory of human vanity over human modesty. Nothing else. I've tried to avoid moments like this in my life, and it was one of the first surprises I had as a writer that I was expected to give talks and presentations whenever a new book came out. Writers write because they don't want to speak, but I was a young man when the media and celebrity culture took off around me. I discovered early that I don't read well from my books, that my tone turns pretentious and Old Testament as soon as I begin reciting words I've written down alone at a desk. Frankly, I find myself near hysteria whenever I listen to my brother and sister writers read portions of their own noble work. This requires a courage I lack, and my dread of boring an audience is close to obsessional. Early on, I decided I would tell stories of my family, friends, and experiences I had as a young Southerner at field in play with the lions of the New York literary world. Later, Hollywood provided a rich vein of golden tales to choose from. My voice is an insufficient, reedy instrument and I still recoil when I hear it played back to me, the same way Sister Sebastian once played back the one sentence I had memorized for a Christmas pageant in sixth grade. But the subject is vanity and its squeaky little pal, humility. My parents did not cotton well to boasting, so I developed an aura of false modesty, so sincere and all-consuming that it still looms as both the phoniest and most *insincere* thing about me. My best friend, the abomination Bernie Schein, still believes it to be a bewildering, effective mask of supreme narcissism. Since Bernie's the most self-inflating narcissist of our times, I must give great weight to his testimony. He has studied me up close for fifty years.

But I agreed to the party and now the day is upon me. I had nothing to do with its planning, its execution, its invitation list, or anything else about it. It fills me with dread, an existential horror and a nightmare coming to pass. I understand my children are all coming and my vengeful brothers and sisters, except for the Conroy family poet, Carol Anne Conroy, who wouldn't come unless I agreed to a second circumcision. The week will begin October 28, when Rob Warley and Jim Hare will be married in our backyard on Battery Creek. Then there'll be a lot of panels and gatherings and friends making a joyful noise about my body and body of work. My wife, the quiet, untrustworthy woman I made vows to, has been a coconspirator in all this. But it will take place in Beaufort, the town that welcomed me home when I rode in following my father's warplane in 1961. It was in Beaufort that I discovered myself, and it provided the stairway into a future that seemed impossible to dream of and terrified me by the force of its ambition. I was not born until I was fifteen years old. It happened here, in Beaufort, in sight of a river's sinuous turn, and the movements of its dolphin-proud tides, its modest, easy grandeur, where I once celebrated being sixteen; now I will turn seventy by its same scrupulous landscape and the place I will one day be buried—in great gratitude and an infinity of joy.

Great love . . .

Pat in the 1970s, when he lived in Atlanta.

The Conroy family. In front: Tom (in mom Peg's lap), Tim (standing next to her). In back: Mike, Jim, Kathy, Pat, Carol.

Pat on Daufuskie Island, 1970.

Pat and Cassandra were married by Judge Alex Sanders,
May 31, 1998.

The Great Santini with Pat on Saint Patrick's Day, 1998.

Pat and Bernie Schein, Pat's closest friend since his
Beaufort High School days.

Pat with his daughter Susannah.

Pat with grandchildren Jack, Katie, and Molly, and his
daughter Megan.

Grave of Pat Conroy at St. Helena Memorial Garden,
March 2016.

On Pat Conroy's Facebook Page on the Day of His Passing

MARCH 4, 2016

We wish he could tell you once again "Hey, out there," but we are the family, the friends, the readers, and we are filled with grief and sadness.

Pat Conroy left this world Friday, March 4, 2016, at 7:42 p.m., surrounded by his family and friends in his Beaufort home overlooking the marshes he so loved.

There are rare people whose very existence makes life bearable for the rest of us for reasons of grace, wisdom, and understanding. Pat was such a man. To say he will be missed is the grandest of understatements.

THE
GREAT
CONROY

‖‖‖‖‖‖‖‖‖‖

A Conversation with Pat Conroy

||||||||||||

MARY ELLEN THOMPSON

✢

BEAUFORT LIFESTYLE, OCTOBER 6, 2015

We think of Pat Conroy as not only a writer, but really, one of the greatest of Southern writers. And he is. Which of us has not read at least one of his books? But the true greatness of Pat Conroy extends so very far beyond the reach of his words. As bedazzling as the rich complexity of the use of language in his novels is, the stories he intersperses in his nonfiction books and blog are the ones that give you the sense of the man, his humanity that has risen over the wounds of his childhood. The amazing boundlessness of his empathy, courage, and arcs of friendships are the finest tributes imaginable to the legions of people with whose lives he has intersected.

Reading a Pat Conroy novel is like being lashed to a mast, and sailing into a story that surrounds you like a blanket of fog. Your primary senses are dulled to anything but the rhetoric and where it will take you; yet in the vast distance you can still sense shrapnel shooting by as the stars of his language explode around you.

Talking with Pat is like facing an immense buffet and trying to choose just what will fit on your plate. We talked about food, exercise, books, and some of the characters he's met along the way. So, come and join us, sit down, eavesdrop on our conversation.

Since food is a legendary affection for Pat, I wondered if his decision to spend time at the gym and get in better shape affected the way he now cooks, and if his cookbook was actually just a masquerade for a book of short stories.

Pat said, "We all know what we should eat, what's healthy; I wrote that cookbook for people who were trying to speed up the dying process. If there was a just and merciful God, a dry martini would have one calorie and a bean sprout would have three thousand.

"In the cookbook are the stories I'd written but not published, I wrote and rewrote them. I loved writing it—no one died, no one was beaten."

We discussed the particular nature of inflicting pain that personal trainers have; Pat agreed, "I'm working out five times a week and something new always hurts; Mina finds ways to torture me."

In his cookbook, Pat comments about his aversion to cilantro, which is a feeling I share. I wondered how he felt about tilapia, which I think became popular on menus at about the same time.

Pat's take? "People look at me like I'm crazy when I say I don't like cilantro; they tell me to try it fresh, or dried, or just out of the garden. I've tried it all those ways; it tastes like soap and I just don't like it. Tilapia? I can't even figure out what tilapia is."

I love the stories Pat tells in the cookbook about the times he unwittingly met some very famous chefs. My favorite was the night Nan Talese was taking him out to dinner to celebrate the launch of *The Prince of Tides*. She didn't realize that the restaurant didn't take credit cards and tried to give the owner/chef her gold bracelets to hold while she went back to the hotel for money, and he wouldn't even consider it. Years later, Pat saw him on television and realized it was Emeril Lagasse.

Pat laughed at the memory. "Nan was wearing an armful of bracelets that were worth a small fortune. I wished I'd had the money to give to him and I could have kept the bracelets! I told her she should have published his first cookbook, but she still thinks he was a dreadful man that night."

Since a conversation with Pat can round more corners than a NASCAR race, it doesn't seem strange that we came to the matter of snakes. He wrote, "My mother, who was no stranger to wildlife, collected poisonous snakes and once told me that a copperhead I caught her for Mother's Day when she was pregnant with my brother Jim was the most thoughtful present she had ever received." I wondered if that seemed out of the ordinary to him.

Pat shook his head. "Not to us, she was the only mother we ever had. I like snakes; I know many people don't, my wife is terrified of them. Mom would get all of us kids banging pots and pans while she went to the other side of the woods and waited for us to scare the snakes out. She would pick them up, she'd pick up a rattlesnake. We all talked about it later and thought it was because she came from a town in Alabama that was rife with snake-handling fundamentalists.''

If you've read any of Conroy, you know that his mother's favorite book of all time was *Gone with the Wind*, and her great love of the book had a profound influence on his life. He was invited by Margaret Mitchell's heirs to write a sequel, but the negotiations and conditions imposed proved too overwhelming and stringent. Because that book had such an impact on him, I wanted to know if he was disappointed that he didn't get to write the sequel. Did he have a strategy for Rhett?

With a sigh, Pat replied, ''I couldn't deal with what they wanted. I wanted to write it because I wanted to dedicate it to my mother. I had some good ideas; it would have been the autobiography of Rhett Butler. I had a plan for Rhett—he was from Charleston, he would have gone to The Citadel.''

''Pat,'' I asked, ''in *Why I Write*, you say, 'My well-used dictionaries and thesauri sing out to me when I write, and all English words are the plainsong of my many-tongued, long-winded ancestors who spoke before me.' I was tickled to see you used 'meretricious' twice in *Beach Music*; are you still a thesaurus user, or after your keeping long lists of words, is your vocabulary now sufficient unto itself?"

Pat handed me one of the brown, well-worn, leather-bound journals that tie with a string of rawhide, and on the left-hand pages were penned, in brown ink, lists of unusual words written in beautiful, and very tiny, script.

He told me, "Sure I still use it, and I keep notebooks. I make a list down the side of the page so the words can inspire me. Language fires me up."

When friends heard I was going to write this story, they asked if I could incorporate some of their questions, and Pat was gracious enough to field them:

SUSAN: I'd ask him how he finds the courage to be so raw and revealing in his writing.

PAT: "It was an accident at first, I didn't realize how many people would be hurt.

"When I wrote *The Boo*, it was the The Citadel, they banned the book. *The Water Is Wide* hurt the city of Beaufort. *The Great Santini* hurt my entire family. But if I didn't tell the truth the way I saw it, I wasn't worth anything as a writer."

CINDY: If you hadn't found literature, what do you
think would have become of your life?

PAT: "I loved teaching. One of the two years I've
never written about were the two years I taught at
Beaufort High School. I don't think I was a very
good teacher, but I loved teaching. I think I would
have gotten good at it, but after Daufuskie no one
would hire me to teach, so it was a good thing that
I liked writing."

PIERCE: Ask him how he came up with the off-the-
wall idea of putting a tiger in *The Prince of Tides*.

PAT: "Happy the Tiger was in a cage at a gas station
in Columbia, South Carolina; I went there to get
gas so I could see him. If you bought gas, you got a
free car wash and while the car was being washed,
you got to throw a chicken neck to the tiger. He
was mean as hell, he probably didn't like being
in a cage outside in the hot South Carolina sun.
They eventually built the zoo in Columbia so that
tiger had a place to go.

"I was living in Rome, the story was in trouble,
it had rapists and murderers and I didn't know
what to do with them. I was out to dinner one
night when I saw a woman in the restaurant and

half of her arm was missing. So I asked her what happened. She had seen a man abusing a tiger at the zoo and wanted to help so she stepped in, and the tiger ripped her arm off. I thought to myself, well, I have a tiger in a barn back there, so that's how he came into the story."

STEVE: How do you know when the end of a story has come, and have any of your characters wanted a sequel?

PAT: "I can feel it coming. In my stories people have been through hell and back; it's time to let them go off into their fictional world.

"When I wrote *The Great Santini*, I planned to have Ben Meecham be the main character in *The Lords of Discipline*, then to have Ben go through his life as the main character of several of the books, but after the movie was made, Hollywood would have owned rights to all those books if Ben was part of them. So I had to change my plan, but it loosened me up."

ELIZABETH: How do you know where to start a book?

PAT: "Usually I don't. Usually it is fizzling around and it starts with the prologue. When I'm finished with the prologue, I can begin in earnest on the novel.

"In *The Great Santini* it was—why did I hate my father? In *The Lords of Discipline*—why I hated the plebe system. In *The Prince of Tides*—why did my sister go crazy?"

After our lovely afternoon I just hugged Pat Conroy, I wanted to thank him with all my heart for all he's done for literature and the truest art of storytelling. Not only are his books exquisite in their mastery, but they have followed the course of his amazing life. I'm hard-pressed to choose between the great descriptive language in his novels, and the stories themselves in the collections. If you've missed reading any of them, get yourselves to the "Pat Conroy at 70" festival, say hello to Pat, buy several of the author's many books, and get them signed!

A Letter to My Grandson on
Sportsmanship and Basketball

||||||||||||||

When I was younger I tried to play basketball, really for Dad, but was just no good at it. I always felt bad that Dad didn't have a kid who shared his passion. In the past few years, my son Jack has really shown promise and has that same obsession Dad had. I don't know what it is like to care that much in a sport, and thought Dad could relate. I asked him for his help and he wrote Jack this letter. I love that they had that connection. One of the things that breaks my heart on a regular basis is the knowledge that Dad will not see him play.

—Megan Conroy

Dear Jack, Beloved Grandson,

Let me tell you about refs and big men and fouls. No one related to you knows the subject so well. First, you must know that I write you as a Citadel point guard who was always the smallest man on the court every college game I played. No one ever worked referees like I did. I made them love me. Often, when I was called for a foul in a game, even when I didn't think I'd committed one, I often said, "Good call, Ref." I know that's never occurred to you in your life and it has rarely occurred to any of you big guys. We little guys have to figure out how to survive. During a practice game, the great Citadel center Dick Martini once stuffed the ball down my throat and sent me flying into the stands. He stood over me in triumph and said, "Hey, stump, don't ever come in here when us big trees are around." I stole the ball from him the next three times down the court when Martini tried to dribble. "Hey, tree," I yelled at him, "don't try to dribble when us little stumps are around, caveman." It's the little guys who are getting you into foul trouble.

Here is my advice. First, a basketball player is cool whenever he or she takes the court. Our team depends on us having clear heads and perfect control of our emotions. We are passionate about the game and it is a fiery, wonderful game, but we never lose our heads even in the midst of the most fierce competition. The great big men are the coolest cats on the planet. Here is what they do, not to foul out. They work on their footwork all the time and they have powers of anticipation and an instinct for moving to the right place at the right time. Learn to dance. Dance every dance at the school prom with your girlfriend, your sisters, or your mother. Learn to be a ballerina on the court. When the big man learns to move, it is the death song for point guards like me. Also, don't try to block every shot. If I saw a big man doing that, I would drive the basket right at them every time. When the big man tries to swat the ball, he goes off balance and then the point guard or the savvy forward eats him alive. Go straight up. Don't lean in. Don't swat. Get in the way. The block will come from your position and height. The ball will come up toward your hand because you're the biggest cat in the litter.

Now we come to the most important thing . . . attitude, demeanor, your presence on the court. Basketball is a sport of inordinate nobility and you owe it your deepest respect. Your character as a man and a player will be judged by how you comport yourself

on the court in victory or defeat. By being gifted in a
sport, you become a role model for everyone around
you, your teammates, your family, your school,
and your community. In sports, you will feel everything . . . elation, despair, wonder, failure. Sports can
teach you everything you need to know about yourself. Carry yourself with immense pride. Sportsmanship is one measure of manhood that you can trust
with absolute certainty. Your grandfather the Great
Santini was the best basketball player the Conroys
ever produced, and I could not carry his jockstrap,
as he reminded me after every game I ever played.
Don Conroy was also the dirtiest basketball player
I ever saw and I didn't want to be a thing like him.
But I could leave the game on the court. I wanted my
opponents to respect me and my teammates to love
me, and they did. I won every sportsmanship trophy on every team I was ever on. I had your same
competitive temperament, but I learned to control it.
I learned to use it to my advantage. I wish to hell I
was a big man like you and I envy the skills Megan
tells me you have, because I was never a natural athlete. But I learned how to use my speed and I could
dribble like few people on earth and I could take it
to the hoop. I loved basketball more than anything

on earth. But I had it under my command. I mastered the part of it I could, but first I had to master the passion and the fury that is the natural condition of the Conroy and the Gigueire males. Work hard on moving fast, going straight up, and sweeping the goddamn boards. Make peace with yourself and our glorious game. I love you with my heart.

Great love . . .

Pat Conroy Talks About the South, His Mother, and *The Prince of Tides*

||||||||||||

FROM A SPEECH DELIVERED AT THE
ANNUAL AMERICAN BOOKSELLERS ASSOCIATION
CONVENTION, 1985

My mother, Southern to the bone, once told me, "All Southern literature can be summed up in these words: 'On the night the hogs ate Willie, Mama died when she heard what Daddy did to Sister.'" She raised me up to be a Southern writer, but it wasn't easy. I didn't grow up in that traditional South. The Marine Corps moved us almost every year of my childhood, and always to Southern towns close to swamps and the sea. I always came as a visitor; I never spent a single day in a hometown. The children of warriors in our country learn the grace and caution that come from a permanent sense of estrangement. I grew up in twenty versions of the South and was part of none of them. At an early age I began to collect the stories that give the native-born a sense of rootedness and place.

My mother thought of my father as half barbarian and half blunt instrument, and she isolated him from his children. When he returned home from work my sister would yell, "Godzilla's home," and the seven children would melt into the secret places of whatever house we happened to be living in at the time. He was no match for my mother's byzantine and remarkable powers of intrigue. Neither were her children. It took me thirty years to realize that I had grown up in my mother's house and not my father's. Like him, I had missed the power source.

In 1984, when I was in the middle of writing *The Prince of Tides*, I drove down to spend two weeks with my mother in a hospital in Augusta, Georgia. She was receiving chemotherapy treatments for the leukemia that would kill her. My mother's favorite character in a book was Scarlett O'Hara and her favorite actress was Vivien Leigh playing Scarlett O'Hara. I grew up thinking that my mother was every bit as pretty as Vivien Leigh and that Scarlett on her best day wouldn't have been a match for my mother. But chemotherapy is not kind to beauty.

One moon-filled night I stayed in my mother's room, to help her through the terrible hours, and she wanted to talk about *The Prince of Tides*. "I'm in your new book, aren't I, Pat?" she asked.

"No," I said.

"Liar," she said. "When you wrote *The Great Santini* you weren't good enough to write about me. I was far more powerful than your father ever was. You just didn't see it."

"I saw it, Mama," I said. "But you're right—I wasn't good enough to write about it."

"I'd like to ask you a favor in the new book, Pat. Don't write about me like this. Make me beautiful. Make me beautiful again."

I knelt beside my mother's bed and said in a voice that I barely recognized, "I'll make you so beautiful, Mama. You made me a writer and I'm going to lift you out of this bed and set you singing and dancing across the pages of my book forever."

"And after you write about my death," my mother said with a smile, "I'd like Meryl Streep to play the role in the movie."

My mother was like a whole civilization of women wrapped up in a single comely package. She was complicated, maddening, irreplaceable. I will never be good enough to write about her. In part, *The Prince of Tides* is a love letter to the dark side of my mother.

I don't think you'd like the portrait, Mama, but wherever you are, I made you beautiful.

Pat Conroy Speaks to
Meredith Maran

||||||||||||||

I've been writing the story of my own life for over forty years. My own stormy autobiography has been my theme, my dilemma, my obsession, and the fly-by-night dread I bring to the art of fiction. Through the years, I've met many writers who tell me with great pride that they consider autobiographical fiction as occupying a lower house in the literary canon. They make sure I know that their imaginations soar into realms and fragments completely invented by them. No man or woman in their pantheon of family or acquaintances has ever taken a curtain call in their own well-wrought and shapely books. Only rarely have I drifted far from the bed where I was conceived.

—Page 1, The Death of Santini, 2013

WHY I WRITE MEMOIR

In 2002 I published my first memoir, *My Losing Season*, about my year as captain of the Citadel basketball team. I wrote it because I wanted to tell the truth about the harsh culture of The Citadel, and my relationship with the coach. That led to writing about the harsh reality of my family.

I waited more than a decade to start writing my second memoir. I'd always wanted to tell the full story of my family, but I had to wait until my parents died. I wanted my readers to know where all my fiction came from. I wanted my memoir to be based not only on what I'd experienced, but also on what my brothers and sisters thought of it all. And I knew I wanted to wait to write it until we had time to age into it—to let it ripen somewhat and to look back on what happened.

When I was researching *The Death of Santini*, I found out some things that absolutely staggered me. My brothers and sisters remembered almost nothing. Each of them remembered only certain things. Much of what they remembered were things I'd written about fictionally. So my "fiction" became part of the memoir.

The same thing happened when I was writing about The Citadel. I went back to get the memories of my classmates about the plebe system and our horrible first year. Most of the guys who survived had simply repressed what happened.

I began to get the thought that some of us are the designated rememberers. Why do we remember? I don't know. But I think that's why memoir interests us—because we're the ones who pass the stories.

FICTION: STRANGER THAN TRUTH

Fiction contains memoir; memoir contains fiction.

Funny things happen when you're writing fiction. Because my father died at the end of my novel *The Great Santini*, when I introduced people to my father in real life, they'd say to him, "Wait! I read about your funeral."

Storytelling is so much more powerful than I'd ever realized. People will take whatever story you tell to be the literal truth. I've had guys I've never seen before come up to me at book readings and say they were my college roommates. I used to think they were just crazies. Now I think it's an imaginative jump they've made, a spark across the night. They somehow actually believe that.

I wrote about a basketball game that took place in 1967. I must have had five thousand people tell me they were there that night. The stadium only holds five thousand! Did I run into every one of them?

I taught in a high school for two years after I was at The Citadel. My brothers and sisters said they've met endless numbers of people who said they were in my classes during that time.

My fiction has become so interwoven with my nonfiction that it has confused everybody, including my brothers and sisters, even though I interviewed them about it before I wrote it. Except for my poet sister Carol, who has disappeared from my life, my siblings and I have been doing panels together about *The Death of Santini*. It's been fascinating to hear their insights.

My brother Jim surprised me during the latest panel we were on. He said, "I can tell the difference between fiction and nonfiction. My father was a total asshole and Pat has always painted him as much too nice. That's fiction!"

ALL'S FAIR IN LOVE AND MEMOIR

My teammates at The Citadel were all concerned when they heard I was working on *My Losing Season*. None of them had ever had a book in their homes. They'd never read another book in their lives. They said, "We don't want you to do a book. You don't make an honest living. All you do is you make shit up about us." Their wives were terrified. Their children were terrified. Everyone was scared to death I'd be making up stuff about them.

I said, "Guys, relax. Here's what you don't know. I'll go over every little thing with y'all. We're going to talk about conversations we had thirty years ago. None of them will be true word-for-word. What we'll aim for is the spirit of those conversations, the flavor of those conversations."

I ended up calling all these guys a million times. I'd call Zipper and I'd tell him, Rube said this; Zipper, do you remember that conversation? Then Zipper would say, Rube's fulla shit. I kept going from one guy to the next. Some guys remembered almost nothing. Some trusted my version of the entire experience. Some guys had amazing memories. I wanted all of them. I told the guys I interviewed, "When the book comes out, and you read it, you need to remember that it's some version of the truth, even though I'm telling you right now it's probably not going to be yours."

The guy I worried about most was the one who suffered the most the year I wrote about in the book. He said, "Conroy, I don't trust you. I read your other books. Look what you did to your old man! If that's what you did to your family in your other books, I can tell you I'm going to hate this one."

After the book came out, that guy stood up and said, "No one is more knowledgeable than I am, and every word in that book was true." As a professional writer I know that that's an impossibility. But it was good to hear.

TRUTH AND LOSS

My sister Carol isn't speaking to me. She barely spoke to me at our mother's funeral. She said we had a toxic family. I said, "No shit. I've been making a living off that toxic family my whole life." What an observation.

Since *The Death of Santini* came out, I haven't heard much from her. I'm sure she's furious about her portrait in the book. I can't blame her. She's a poet, and she's very private. Her privacy means everything to her. She's fiercely guarded. You will not find her giving interviews to anybody about anything.

The only time she's broken that rule was for an odd CNN Conroy Thanksgiving special when Dad was still alive. He had cancer. It was his last year alive. We all got together, and Carol finally accepted me and Dad and the family for what we were.

The reunion was phony. Everyone knew it. It was the most uncomfortable scene since the Pilgrims sat down with the Native Americans after Plymouth Rock. I watched the show and I thought, My God in heaven, what a travesty of a festive moment. It was so painful.

I've thought about this a lot. When you write memoir, who are you hurting? It's always been the great taboo: hurting your parents, hurting your family, hurting your children—although I tell my children I can't wait to write about their hellion teenage years when they dated the most hideous boys in America, just to torture me.

If I'm writing a portrait of my family and I don't talk about the effect of that family on Carol, my beloved sister, if I don't talk about how her childhood ruined her life, I'd be a liar and an unfit witness for the family I've been writing about. I decided that if I'm going to write about this, I want to write the truth as I know it, as I lived it.

TRUTH: RELATIVE

People who read my memoirs ask me how I know what's true and what's not true. I don't worry about it too much. I understand memoir and fiction, and I understand that there's making-up going on with both.

I've seen memoirists who go nuts for absolute scrupulous word-for-word truth telling. It's an impossible standard. If you have to write it perfectly, the story won't be told. Here's what I know: If a story is not told, it's the silence around that untold story that ends up killing people. The story can open a secret up to the light.

When you write a memoir, you want it to be as true as you can make it. With fiction you have a much larger body of water to play in. But I have to admit this right away: I'm swimming in dangerous water when I talk about the difference between memoir and fiction. I've often intermingled the two.

Trying to figure out where the truth lies is one of the perils of writing memoir.

TRUTH: HARD TO BELIEVE

I had trouble with *The Great Santini* because my very proper editor said, in her British accent, "Pat, it's simply not believable that a father would treat a son in this extraordinary way." I had to clean up the book to make it believable to people who went to Harvard.

I was light on my father in that book. I wasn't yet prepared to say he beat us half to death and left us in the driveway. I had trouble getting people to believe me. There was an article in *Atlanta Magazine* saying that I'd made the whole thing up. My father told them, "If anything, I was too good a father. My son has a vivid imagination."

I wrote a letter to the editor, saying Yeah, I made the whole thing up. My father was a Carmelite nun. I used my imagination to make everything up.

MEMOIR MATTERS

Memoir has been necessary for my life. I've found writers whose voices I can trust. In their memoirs they came out and told me things I needed to know about how to live a life. If not for those writers telling me how to look for truth in life, how to know it's there when you find it, I don't know who I'd be.

WRITE ANOTHER ONE? I THINK NOT

I'm glad I made it out of that last memoir alive, except for Carol. I can't tell you how much I regret losing my sister, and I can't say she's wrong to have those feelings. I suffered over that. I suffer still. When you write memoir, that's part of the bargain you make with God and the devil.

On My Paris Days

||||||||||||

GOURMET, AUGUST 2006

On the last days I would ever feel like a young man, I went to live in Paris to finish the novel I was writing at the time, *The Lords of Discipline*. While attending The Citadel, I had gone into an uncontrollable rapture when I read Ernest Hemingway's *A Moveable Feast*. He made the city of Paris glisten with a romantic luster it has never lost for me, and I could think of no finer way to spend a part of my life than by writing a book in the storied, uncapturable city of literature and light.

My decision to go to Paris was both whimsical and spontaneous. Houghton Mifflin had just assigned me my third editor at the publishing company, the brilliant, young, and fastidious Jonathan Galassi, who was destined to be one of the greatest editors ever to walk the streets of New York. I had liked everything about Mr. Galassi until he called to tell me he had accepted a grant and a sabbatical to live in Paris and Rome for a year while he translated the essays of Eugenio Montale. It irritated me that I had never heard of Montale, but Jon was that kind of intellectual. His mind was the most exciting country he would ever visit. But it amazed me that he would be in Europe and unavailable when my novel made its shy appearance the following year.

"It's an outrage," I said on the phone. "It's a complete betrayal of our relationship as novelist and editor, Harvard boy."

"It's a done deal, Pat," he answered in his calm, mannerly editor's voice, which contained all the passion of a bivalve. "I've already accepted both the grant and the sabbatical."

"You can't do this to me," I said. "You just can't do it."

"Why don't you go with us?" he asked. "I'll work something out with Houghton Mifflin."

So I spent a cold and glorious winter in an overcast Paris, where it rained almost every day. Susan and Jonathan Galassi helped me find the reasonable, finely located Grand Hôtel des Balcons, just steps away from the Place de l'Odéon and the Luxembourg Gardens, in the sixth arrondissement. My concierge was a surly, imposing woman, but she brightened when I paid her the first month's rent, and she put me in a garret on the top floor with her other artistes. My room had a balcony, a sink, a bed, a very good desk and chair, and a view of the Eiffel Tower. The room cost me seven dollars a night, and every time I paid my rent, I felt I had just robbed a bank. The room was not only cheap, it came with a breakfast of croissants, butter, jam, and coffee. It was easy to fall in love with morning when it started off with such a simple but delicious feast.

From the very beginning, the writing went well. I learned to work with the French doors thrown open to the balcony, which also served as my refrigerator and wine cooler and cheese drawer. I learned to write to the rhythm and pace of French rain, and I could feel the story unfolding inside me as I filled up yellow legal pads in a language that few in the hotel could read. Though my French did not improve, I would feel the English language beginning to well up inside me as it formed itself into chandeliers and peacocks and burnished cutlery. I could feel the whole city doing its subtle, cunning work on me, as I had begun to write sentences that sounded more like stained-glass windows than clear-eyed explanations of the events at hand. Before that moment, I didn't know a writer's style could change, and that a strange, fascinating city could hasten the process along. Each time I walked out of the Hôtel des Balcons, I could turn in any direction and find a Paris of mysteries both heady and disquieting. In my mind, I could take along the novel I was working on. I could wander the inimitable greenness of the Luxembourg Gardens with characters who knew how to clean M1 rifles and spoke in Southern accents.

If I veered right when I exited my hotel, I would soon be walking beside the river toward the islands of the Seine, or drifting through the imposing college buildings of the Sorbonne, watching the impeccably dressed diners enter La Tour d'Argent. Both day and night, I walked Paris as though it were duty and opportunity and chance of a lifetime. My mother had made me hunger for culture from the day I was born, and now I found myself a temporary citizen in a city that had given the world its most beautiful language and writers passionate enough and gifted enough to write books that were deathless and breathtaking in their execution. It was the winter I read Marcel Proust's *In Search of Lost Time* from beginning to end, then visited his grave at Père Lachaise Cemetery and had lunch there. When Parisians spoke to each other in restaurants and cafés, it sounded to me as though they were passing orchids and roses through their lips. I spoke French like a donkey, and no amount of mimicry or fakery could make any of the French think differently. There was not a French word I could not make potted meat of as it fell to the floor from the meat grinder of my tongue. There was not a single district in the city I could enter without becoming a laughingstock when I ordered a brioche or a dozen escargots.

In the evening I would often join Jonathan and Susan Galassi for dinner at a restaurant they had selected with great care for both its quality and relative cheapness. They were living in the lovely Hôtel des Grandes Écoles, across the street from the sawmill where Ernest and Hadley Hemingway had lived when they were young and poor and in love with Paris and each other.

I had never met a couple like the Galassis in my

life. The sheer range of their education and intellectual passions bedazzled me. Often we would begin
our evenings with a slow walk down the Rue Mouf-
fetard, a profligate market street with endless stores
overflowing with fruits and cheeses and vegetables of
every sort. To me, it looked as if the farmers of France
had delivered everything their fields could grow to
this amazing, spilling-down street where carts reeling
with tomatoes, avocados, cauliflowers, and grapes
stood taller than I did. Sometimes, we would stop and
buy food for our lunches the next day.

That winter we ate cheaply. That winter we ate
like princes of the earth. The Galassis would study
the menus of brasseries and cafés that fell within the
realms of our limited budgets. By the light of candles,
I ate sweetbreads and lamb kidneys for the first time
and learned the extraordinary range of pâtés and
the names of fish that swam in the Mediterranean.
Meanwhile, we would talk about the work we had
done that day. Susan Galassi, as finely boned and
pretty as the woman etched into the bottle of White
Shoulders perfume, would speak of her progress
on her doctoral dissertation, which she was calling
Picasso: Variations of the Old Masters. One night she
took us to Delacroix's studio; afterward, we ended

the evening by toasting each other with Armagnac, a rougher kind of cognac that they had discovered on their honeymoon. As we lifted our glasses, tuxedoed waiters flowed past us at Les Deux Magots, where Sartre and Beauvoir had once argued philosophy. We pledged our friendship to be immortal and unbreakable. I felt like an artist, bright and footloose on the boulevards.

All day I would write. It came to me in a flood tide, like it has never come before or since. At night I would attend concerts with the Galassis, or the opera, and I would roam the Louvre and other art galleries with Susan whenever I could. She could take a painting, any painting, and contrive a love story to it in words that sprang out of her with vivacity and charm. When she was confronted by a masterpiece she had given her heart to, the words came out slowly, and I could watch the conversion that has always united art and prayer. To Susan, an art gallery was her cathedral, her sacristy, her confessional, and her life's work. My great luck lay in her openness of heart as she shared the secrets of canvases I had never heard of, and her eyes appraised the work of artists through miles and miles of Parisian hallways. Art, like the Seine, was just another river to fall in love with in Paris.

Before they left for Rome for the final months of their sabbatical, Jonathan made a long-distance phone call to Houghton Mifflin to get permission to take me to one fine restaurant in Paris. Neither of us had produced great dividends for the company at that time, but he received permission to eat in a nice restaurant, though not a fine one. We chose a celebrated French place called Dodin-Bouffant, which was known for its seafood, for one of our last nights together. I ordered a half-dozen Bélon oysters because I did not want to return to the States without ever having tasted the famous Bélons, and they were priced like amethysts even in those faraway days. They were cold, superb, and salty, and a Chablis Premier Cru that Jon had selected accompanied them to perfection. As the meal progressed, I remember passing around plates that contained Dover sole, turbot, and a scallop dish that approached sublimity. The meal ended with a cheese cart, then Armagnac, and then talk turned to our meeting in Rome, when the novel would be finished and I would present a manuscript to Jonathan in payment to him for the ineffable gift of Paris.

For over a month I was in Paris alone, writing about characters who moved through the streets and houses and barracks of Charleston, South Carolina. The weather began to change slowly, and I could feel spring in its ballet slippers making its shy appearance onstage in the Luxembourg Gardens. The fruit and vegetables on the market street of the Rue de Seine near my hotel grew brighter and fresher every day. The chestnut trees began to bloom, and I had never known those magnificent trees were one of the glories of Paris. Each day I wrote a letter or a postcard to my three daughters in Atlanta. I would go to American Express to mail them, stopping by the Louvre each time I went. I received a letter from my friend Cliff Graubart, telling me that he and another friend, Frank Smith, were going to meet me in Paris in the middle of May. The three of us would drive my manuscript down to Rome. "Plan to have the greatest time of your life," Cliff wrote, and I so promised myself.

The day before I finished *The Lords of Discipline*, I wrote the last chapter of the novel in a single sitting. One cadet had betrayed his three roommates and that cadet was my favorite character in the book. But novels take on a life of their own and sometimes drift out of the writer's control. I now know that could happen even when the writer was living in Paris. Now, Atlanta was calling me away from this enchanting, provocative city, a part of which would live inside me forever.

When I met Frank and Cliff at the Gare du Nord the next day, I was greeting one of the best parts of my Atlanta life. Before we left Paris, we rented a white Simca and bought three wineglasses, a corkscrew, paper plates, knives and forks, and paper napkins. At a charcuterie near the Hôtel des Balcons, we bought our lunch for the first day, consisting of two cheeses, Chaource and Camembert, a hard sausage, a duck pâté, a baguette, and a bottle of Rosé d'Anjou. I packed my seven-hundred-page manuscript as carefully as though I were transporting the Book of Kells across hostile borders. While putting it in my suitcase, it struck me as a very bad idea that I had resisted making a copy of the book because of the exorbitant price. We loaded up the Simca with our luggage and set out for Rome with Frank, driving out of the sixth arrondissement, my home for five months.

We took all back roads through the peerless French countryside, through villages that were breathtaking to behold and past farms that were hundreds of years old. For lunch, we stopped and ate beneath an arched bridge that crossed over a swift stream where trout hunted mayflies. A herd of sheep grazed on a nearby hillside. We ate slowly, spreading the pâté on pieces of the baguette after Frank had cut sausage and cheese with his well-kept Swiss Army knife, and Cliff had cooled the wine in the stream before opening it.

"This must be the most beautiful spot in Europe," Frank said.

"You'll say that ten thousand more times before we get to Rome," I told him.

Lunch became our joy and our specialty. We searched out locally produced cheeses, olives, sausages, and breads. We tried to buy wines made in the same district where we purchased them. We lunched on a pier overlooking the city of Geneva, near a waterfall looking at a monastery near Brig, Switzerland, and in the ruins of a portico that extended out into the waters of Lake Maggiore, in Italy. At Maggiore, as we feasted on grapes and olives and prosciutto, we agreed we had come to the most beautiful place on earth.

At one of the beaches near Portofino, Cliff and Frank decided that they wanted to join the crowds who were swimming in the ocean. I issued a warning that I had been robbed my first time in Rome, but the day was hot, and Cliff and Frank were determined they were not going back to America without having swum in the Mediterranean. We locked the car, changed into our bathing suits, and, despite my misgivings, were soon by the water's edge. Frank and Cliff swam out into deep water as I remained in the shallows and tried to keep an eye on the car. I soon grew fascinated by the sight of an Italian man lifting black sea urchins out of the water, disemboweling them, and eating them raw.

When we returned to the car, Cliff was the first to notice that a thief had kicked in one of the windows and robbed us. Frank lost his camera and Cliff lost a gold watch his father had given him. I went weak at the knees when I remembered that my manuscript was in a suitcase in the backseat. If the robber had reached in and stolen all the luggage, my life would be very different today. I could easily have lost five years of my life. But he was discriminating in his desires and had no need for a novel written in a strange tongue.

On the evening we entered Rome, we rented a cheap hotel room near the Spanish Steps and met Jonathan and Susan Galassi for dinner at the Trattoria del Pantheon da Fortunato. I handed my novel to Jonathan, and the next day he called to tell me that he would accept it if I would make one major change. When we met, I agreed on the spot to the change, and we shook hands. For the next two days Jonathan and Susan took us around to explore a city they had come to love as much as they had Paris. Here, in a Roman setting, they seemed even more cosmopolitan, sophisticated, and enlightened than ever, and they treated Cliff and Frank as though they had known them all their lives. Because of fate, the Galassis had given me the city of Paris, which led to Frank and Cliff's discovery of Europe.

On my last night in Rome, I watched the sunset with the Galassis on their terrace in Trastevere. I was full of emotion and felt lucky to have such friends. The sun darkened the enameled, coppery city below us. I raised a glass of wine to toast my friends before I went back to my life in Atlanta, the one I was born to live.

When I had first gone to Paris, almost twenty years before, I had read F. Scott Fitzgerald's broken-down, elegiac novel *Tender Is the Night.* I had always loved his dedication to Sara and Gerald Murphy in the book, and that is what I wanted to convey as I toasted friends and Europe good-bye. "Many fêtes," I tried to say. I don't think anyone heard me, but they all caught the mood of what I meant.

A Letter to the Editor of the

Charleston Gazette

||||||||||||||

OCTOBER 24, 2007

I received an urgent e-mail from a high school student named Makenzie Hatfield of Charleston, West Virginia. She informed me of a group of parents who were attempting to suppress the teaching of two of my novels, *The Prince of Tides* and *Beach Music*. I heard rumors of this controversy as I was completing my latest filthy, vomit-inducing work. These controversies are so commonplace in my life that I no longer get involved. But my knowledge of mountain lore is strong enough to know the dangers of refusing to help a Hatfield of West Virginia. I also do not mess with McCoys.

I've enjoyed a lifetime love affair with English teachers, just like the ones who are being abused in Charleston, West Virginia, today. My English teachers pushed me to be smart and inquisitive, and they taught me the great books of the world with passion and cunning and love. Like your English teachers, they didn't have any money either, but they lived in the bright fires of their imaginations, and they taught because they were born to teach the prettiest language in the world. I have yet to meet an English teacher who assigned a book to damage a kid. They take an unutterable joy in opening up the known world to their students, but they are dishonored and unpraised because of the scandalous paychecks they receive. In my travels around this country, I have discovered that America hates its teachers, and I could not tell you why. Charleston, West Virginia, is showing clear signs of really hurting theirs, and I would be cautious about the word getting out.

In 1961, I entered the classroom of the great Eugene Norris, who set about in a thousand ways to change my life. It was the year I read *The Catcher in the Rye*, under Gene's careful tutelage, and I adore that book to this very day. Later, a parent complained to the school board, and Gene Norris was called before the board to defend his teaching of this book. He asked me to write an essay describing the book's galvanic effect on me, which I did. But Gene's defense of *The Catcher in the Rye* was so brilliant and convincing in its sheer power that it carried the day. I stayed close to Gene Norris till the day he died. I delivered a eulogy at his memorial service and was one of the executors of his will.

Few in the world have ever loved English teachers as I have, and I loathe it when they are bullied by know-nothing parents or cowardly school boards.

About the novels your county just censored: *The Prince of Tides* and *Beach Music* are two of my darlings which I would place before the altar of God and say, "Lord, this is how I found the world you made." They contain scenes of violence, but I was the son of a Marine Corps fighter pilot who killed hundreds of men in Korea, beat my mother and his seven kids whenever he felt like it, and fought in three wars. My youngest brother, Tom, committed suicide by jumping off a fourteen-story building; my French teacher ended her life with a pistol; my aunt was brutally raped in Atlanta; eight of my classmates at The Citadel were killed in Vietnam; and my best friend was killed in a car wreck in Mississippi last summer.

Violence has always been a part of my world. I write about it in my books and make no apology to anyone. In *Beach Music*, I wrote about the Holocaust and lack the literary powers to make that historical event anything other than grotesque.

People cuss in my books.

People cuss in my real life. I cuss, especially at Citadel basketball games. I'm perfectly sure that Steve Shamblin and other teachers prepared their students well for any encounters with violence or profanity in my books, just as Gene Norris prepared me for the profane language in *The Catcher in the Rye* forty-eight years ago.

The world of literature has everything in it, and it refuses to leave anything out. I have read like a man on fire my whole life because the genius of English teachers touched me with the dazzling beauty of language. Because of them I rode with Don Quixote and danced with Anna Karenina at a ball in Saint Petersburg and lassoed a steer in *Lonesome Dove* and had nightmares about slavery in *Beloved* and walked the streets of Dublin in *Ulysses* and made up a hundred stories in *The Arabian Nights* and saw my mother killed by a baseball in *A Prayer for Owen Meany*. I've been in ten thousand cities and have introduced myself to a hundred thousand strangers in my exuberant reading career, all because I listened to my fabulous English teachers and soaked up every single thing those magnificent men and women had to give. I cherish and praise them and thank them for finding me when I was a boy and presenting me with the precious gift of the English language.

The school board of Charleston, West Virginia, has sullied that gift and shamed themselves and their community. You've now entered the ranks of censors, book banners, and teacher haters, and the word will spread. Good teachers will avoid you as though you had cholera. But here is my favorite thing: Because you banned my books, every kid in that county will read them, every single one of them. Because book banners are invariably idiots, they don't know how the world works—but writers and English teachers do.

I salute the English teachers of Charleston, West Virginia, and send my affection to their students. West Virginians, you've just done what history warned you against—you've riled a Hatfield.

A Lowcountry Heart

||||||||||||

In 1961, the Marine Corps sent my father orders that would send the Conroy family rocketing toward a destiny we were never supposed to have. When our child-laden car entered Beaufort County as we crossed over the pristine waters of the Combahee River, I caught my first unforgettable view of the Great Salt Marsh. It was the year I learned to water-ski in the Broad River, that I attended my first oyster roast at a house on Port Royal Sound, and that a Marine colonel took me on a fishing trip to an uninhabited sea island called Fripp. It was during this enchanting, unforgettable year that I developed a Lowcountry heart.

When I began to write my books, I thought I carried the comeliness of the Lowcountry deep inside me. Its beauty was a shining thing and a living thing that would never leave me as long as I was true to that starry, everlasting river-fed country of my art. That was Beaufort's gift to me. I can't write an English sentence without breaking out in song praising the everlasting summons of these shining sea islands we call home. When I came to Beaufort I had struck upon a land so beautiful I had to hunt for other words that ached with the joyous, carnal charms of the green marshes that seemed to be the source of all life. I would watch the breath of earth move the high tides of spring as shrimp boats inched out to sea at first light. On the beaches, loggerhead turtles would emerge in the fire-struck linens (maybe havens?) of full moons to deposit glistening, sea-born eggs into funnels of beach-sculpted sands as herds of white-tailed deer drifted like smoke through palmetto forests. Osprey would impale the mullets from golf course lagoons, and cobia would lace their way through salt rivers in their own madness to spawn as blue herons hunted in perfect stillness, as hundreds of thousands of horseshoe crabs gathered to mate in the shallows along Land's End. This is the homeplace the Marine Corps brought me to as a boy. In my stories, my currents are shad-honored and dolphin-laced. They bring the sure knowledge that the lord of waters watches over them in the deepest pride of creation.

Ten years ago, I stood on a balcony of an endangered house that sat on the beachfront of Fripp Island. The man standing beside me was from the Upcountry. He was well-spoken and deeply religious. He and I watched a full moon rise out of the Atlantic. Neither of us spoke a word. The moon laid down a prayer cloth of light that stretched out for a thousand miles of seawater.

The man spoke first. "I'm afraid of dying," he said.

"Because you'll miss all this," I said.

"No," he said. "I'm worried that heaven's not going to be this pretty."

I knew the soul of that man by the words he spoke. And I know the souls of the people who have gathered here tonight. We are here because of our love of this incomparable portion of the earth. We are here because we have Lowcountry hearts.

Pat Conroy's Citadel Speech

||||||||||||

General Grinalds; the Board of Visitors; Lt. Col. Thomas Nugent Courvoisie, The Boo, and my first book; Greg and Mary Wilson Smith, The Citadel family who did more than anyone else to bring me back to my Citadel family; Skip Wharton; Rogers Harrell, member of the Class of '01 [who] lost his father last year, and his father will not be able to hand him his diploma, but members of the Class of '71 have rallied here because of the love of that father. Class of 2001, listen up, I don't have much time. They don't give you much time for graduation speeches. Because of various aspects of my character and fate, I did not get to address the Corps of Cadets in the last century. There were many years when I thought that Saddam Hussein or Jane Fonda had a better chance of addressing this class than I did.

In 1979, the year most of y'all were born, I was finishing up *The Lords of Discipline* and I tried to think of a line or words that would sum up better than anything how I felt and how other people feel about this college. I wanted it to be something ringing and affirmative, something true, something that would be true for every person who has ever gone through the long gray line. I came up with this line: "I wear the ring."

I think it is the best line I have ever written and best English sentence I am capable of writing. I love that phrase; I love that sentence. Thirty-four years ago, I sat in this field house. My mother and father, my six brothers and sisters, sitting in the audience as your parents are sitting now. My parents—it was their proudest day. My mother wept when I came off [the stage] that day. She wept so hard, and I said, "Mom, what's wrong?" And she said, "Son, you are the first person in my family who has ever graduated from college, and you did it at The Citadel." And she said, "The best college in America."

Let me tell you something about that mother. Here is my mother's socioeconomic status exactly. Everything you need to know about my family [you can learn] from her mother's family name. My grandfather, Jasper Catholic Peek; his brother, Cicero. Then there's Vashtye, Taleatha, Clyde, Pluma. And my favorite—I was cleaning up a grave with my grandmother, Stanny, and I came across this name, "Jerry Mire Peek"—okay, that's Jerry Mire—M-I-R-E Peek. And I said, "Stanny, who is he named after?" And she said, "He is named after the prophet, Jerrymire."

My father was a different case. My father, six feet, three inches, 230-pound Marine Corps fighter pilot, knuckles dragging along the ground when he walked. When he was dying, I interviewed Dad. I said, "Dad, tell me about what it was like in the war."

He told me about coming off the aircraft carrier *Sicily* in Korea. His was the first squadron that got there, and they said, "Keep the Koreans north of the Nakdong River." So he dove down—the first plane the North Koreans had seen—he dove down toward the enemy. I said, "How did you do, Dad?"

He said, "I did pretty good, son." He said, "I had a good sign—they were running. It's good when you see the enemy running. There was another good sign, son."

"What's that, Dad?"

"They were on fire."

That was the man who dandled me on his knee when I was a young boy—the Great Santini. I once introduced my father when I was giving a talk like this, and I said, "My father decided to go in the Marine Corps when he found out that his IQ was the temperature of this room."

My father got up right behind me. He stared down at the audience and he said, "My God, it's hot in here . . . it must be at least 165 degrees."

These were the people who raised me, the people who inspired me. They sent me to this college. They did not ask me where I wanted to go. Both of them wanted [me] to go here. My father applied to this college. I did not. I never saw an application. Never signed an application, but ended up here in 1963 for Hell Week. I remember Hell Week. I don't know how you did it, kids, but they did it good back then, I want to tell you. And after Hell Night, I remember going there—it was a vivid experience—an upperclassman came and said, "Mr. Conroy, you look tired, exhausted. Why don't you come to my room and just hang out for a while."

The next thing I knew I was hanging from the pipe

in his room. And I realized that I had come to a place that has etched itself on me, etched itself on my character. I have written more about my college than any writer in American history. My book will be coming out next year—it will be the third book I have written about this college. And I write about it because I cannot keep away from it . . . the experience, it's so fresh and fiery on my imagination. And because it's a great relationship, I wanted to tell you something seriously, I wanted to tell my Citadel family how I got involved in the great war of bringing women to this college. After I wrote *The Lord of Discipline* in 1980 and the reaction of this school, kids, Conroy ain't stupid. This is a tough place. And I said, "Okay, I have gotten through that," and I was retiring from the field for the rest of my life. I was speaking in colleges in the Northeast. I spoke at Harvard, the Rhode Island School of Design. And then I was looking down at the next college I was supposed to speak at, and, to my amazement, it was the Coast Guard Academy. Ladies and gentlemen, the Class of 2001, you probably think I speak at military colleges a lot, but after *The Lords of Discipline*, the invitations—I got one invitation from VMI. The man who invited me was fired the next day. So I called my wife, and I said, "There's the Coast Guard Academy. I cannot possibly speak there."

She said, "Yeah, they pay you money . . ."

So I went to the Coast Guard Academy and was met by the guy who invited me, and he said, "Mr. Conroy, I had no idea inviting you would be such a stir." He said, "The commandant told me if you said anything that irritated him, he would fire me even though I had tenure."

So I said, "What do you think I'm going to do, call for the dissolution of the American armed forces?" I said, "This will be great."

The commandant flew up from Washington. He sat there stern-faced. I like the way generals can be stern. So he was sitting there stern-faced, and I talked to the group, but first of all, I had gone to talk to the freshmen. I talked to these freshmen, and I looked out there, and 25 percent of them were women. I said, "What are you girls doing here? Are you crazy? Are you nuts?"

And one of them there, the woman who was leading me around, said, "Sir, they let women in the academies in 1974."

And I said to these freshmen girls, "Is it as horrible for y'all as it was for me when I was a freshman?"

A couple of them go—you can't say anything naturally—but a couple of these young women went [Conroy nods his head].

I talked to the Coast Guard Academy that night. I had a ball. I want to tell y'all something—I can talk to a corps of cadets. I talked to them about what happened to me at The Citadel. We roared with laughter. Military colleges—we have common experiences; we share common things. When they took me to the plane the next day, the four women—I asked them—I said, "What are you going to do when you get out of here?"

One of the women said, "Fly an attack helicopter, sir."

"No kidding. What are you going to do?"

"Drive a ship, sir."

So they helped me off then, these four accursed Coast Guard Academy women. And right before I got on the plane, one said, "How'd you like the Coast Guard Academy?"

"I loved it."

Then one of them said, "How'd you like us, sir? How'd you like the women at the Coast Guard Academy?"

I said, "I loved y'all. What's not to like? You're sharp cadets—funny, smart."

One of them then said, the trap then being set, "Mr. Conroy, when a woman applies at The Citadel, will you help her out? Will you support her? She's not going to have much."

I said, "Listen, gals, you don't know The Citadel. That is *never* going to happen in my lifetime. It's not even a chance and you just don't know The Citadel."

And one of the women said, "Mr. Conroy, you don't know women."

In the early nineties I received a letter from one of those accursed Coast Guard women. "Mr. Conroy, the first woman has applied to The Citadel. We remember your talk. Your talk is famous at the Coast Guard Academy. We especially remember you talking about your time on the honor courts, how much that meant to you. How much that changed you. How much that set your character. And we know because you promised to support the first woman that we can count on you because, like you, we have an honor system we believe in. Her name is Shannon Faulkner. And we know you'll do your duty."

I tore that letter up. I said, "These women are going to get me killed." But I'm a Citadel man, and they mentioned the honor code. And there's a lot wrong with me, Class of 2001, except this—I know what the meaning of "is" is.

While writing this latest book, *My Losing Season*, I interviewed all the basketball players, the boys I loved from this gymnasium . . . I adored them. They did not know it. I went back to meet all of them, but one meeting changed my life. I went back to see Al Kroboth, center, Class of 1969, a POW, a Marine in Vietnam. I sat him down, and I said, "Al, you got to tell me about being a POW. You got to tell me everything, but I'm a novelist—you got to let me know how it feels."

"Can I have my wife, Patty, be with me?"

"Sure."

An interview I thought would take an hour, took seven. And I said, "Al, history is going to come between us." And history is going come all over this, Class of 2001. And I said, "Al, I was a draft dodger. I was a Vietnam protester during the war . . . you need to know this before we talk."

He said, "Conroy, you did what you did. I did what I did. I'm fine."

Then he proceeds to tell me about the most harrowing Vietnam experience I've ever heard of where he is shot down. He wakes up with an AK-47 pointed at his face. He has a broken back, a shattered scapula. They tell him to get up, and Al Kroboth, who is in South Vietnam, in the jungle, walks barefoot at night for three months through the Vietnam jungle. It is the most horrible, tortured thing I have ever heard about in my life.

I said, "Al, how did you make it? How'd you do the pain, the leeches, the boils, the bites—everything?" I said, "How'd you make it?"

Al Kroboth looks at me and says, "The plebe system. I made it because of the plebe system. I made it because I'm a Citadel man."

He gets along. He's in terrible, terrible confinement in North Vietnam. Then I said, "Tell me when you got out, Al. Tell me how it felt."

He talked about the plane landing. Al's a Marine, like the general. And Al is standing there. "I didn't feel anything, Conroy. And then the plane, I saw it go down to the end of the field, and I saw it turn, and I saw the American flag." And as Al Kroboth said he saw the American flag, he wept. His wife wept. Then I wept.

He said then the plane takes off and all of the POWs are in this plane, and he says he's not feeling anything. And then the pilot comes on and says, "Feet wet. Feet wet. We have left North Vietnamese territory."

And Al Kroboth weeps again, and his wife weeps.

[He said] the North Vietnamese told them that Americans hated the war. They were hated. That they were considered war criminals. So when Al landed, and all of the other POWs in the Philippines, they got a hero's welcome from ten thousand people . . . he was shocked when he walked through that crowd, across a red carpet, and a little girl sitting on her father's shoulders handed him a piece of paper. He didn't look at it until he got on the bus. And in this childish scrawl, this girl had written, "Greater love than this, no man hath."

And Al Kroboth broke again. His wife broke. I broke.

Then Al, on the tenth floor being debriefed, he gets a call that there's a Citadel man waiting for him down in the lobby, so he takes an officer down there, and he goes down to the lobby, and Johnny Vaughan, who had been a cheerleader on my basketball team— Johnny used to jump up and down for me and Al— Johnny Vaughan is waiting for Al Kroboth. And he gets down there, and they embrace, and then Johnny says, "Al, I heard you lost your Citadel ring."

And Al said, "The Vietcong stole it."

And then, what to me is one of the great moments in Citadel history—Johnny Vaughan took off his Citadel ring and said, "I'm not letting you go back to America without wearing a Citadel ring."

Al said, "No, Johnny, I can't do it. I've lost too much weight. I'll lose it."

Johnny said, "No, no. Listen to me, I'm not letting you go back to America without wearing a Citadel ring."

And he took Al's hand, and he put his ring on Al Kroboth's hand.

Class of 2001, I brought an audiovisual aid for you today. I wanted to bring the type of alumni you are capable of turning yourselves into. I would like Al Kroboth and Johnny Vaughan to stand up and meet the Class of 2001. Where are you guys? [Mr. Kroboth and Mr. Vaughan stand to the audience's applause.]

In closing, Class of 2001, I cannot thank y'all enough for doing this for me. I did not exactly pencil this speech into my schedule of coming attractions, and you do me the highest honor by bringing me fully into my Citadel family. And I was trying to think of something I can do because a graduation speaker needs to speak of time—time passing. Usually, I tell graduation classes I want them to think of me on their fortieth birthday, but I got something else I want to do for y'all because I'm so moved at what you've done for me. I would like to invite each one of you in the Class of 2001 to my funeral, and I mean that. I will not be having a good day that day . . . but I have told my wife and my heirs that I wanted the Class of 2001 to have an honored place whenever my funeral takes place. And I hope as many of you will come as you possibly can, because I want you to know how swift time is, and there is nothing as swift—and you know this—from the day you walked into Lesesne Gateway until this day—a heartbeat, an eye blink. This is the way life is. It is the only great surprise in life.

So I'm going to tell you how to get to my funeral. You walk up . . . You find the usher waiting outside, and here's your ticket . . . You put up your Citadel ring. Let them check for the 2001, and each one of you, I want you to say this before you enter the church at which I'm going to be buried. You tell them, "I wear the ring."

Thank you so much.

Farewell Letter

||||||||||||||||

BY BERNIE SCHEIN

❧

MARCH 8, 2016

My dearest Pat,

I know we've said good-bye to each other more times in the last several weeks than either one of us might have imagined only a short time ago. Such is the nature of the obsessive-compulsive Jew who can't let go and an Irish Catholic blowhard with a heart so big I imagine it now dwarfing the universe. They'll love you up there: Peg and Don, Stannie, Mom and Dad, Gene, Doug, Tommy, Nancy Jane, all your loved ones. You're regaling all of them right now, I have no doubt, they're so happy to see you.

You had to have been dying to see them, since you did.

Frankly, my guess is your arrival on the scene at St. Peter's has even God opening His arms with a grin to match yours, and a heartfelt embrace. If He hadn't needed a good laugh and some personality up there, you'd probably still be here driving all of us crazy.

When we last said good-bye to each other, I told you my heart and soul will always be with you, as yours will always be inside me. The advantage there, as I've reminded you on countless occasions, is yours. Needless to say, mine will make you a better person.

Your love, so inspired, so generous and warm and such a pain in the ass, that's what I'll miss, Bubba. That's what I'll miss. Your humor, which is so pathetic. Please, some new material, you've got time up there, mentally telegraph it to my imagination. God, did we laugh.

And lord, did we cry. My friend, my friend. My soul mate, my inspiration, my muse, my devil's advocate. You care so much, I feel it. Yes, you could be a jerk, we all know that, but in the final analysis, when all is said and done . . . I remember we were talking to James

Dickey's sister, Pat Dickey, in your study in Atlanta, about "character," about seeing people accurately. At that moment you challenged me to look around your library and tell you the most important book of your youth. (*Famous All Over Town* had not yet been written.) You're laughing at that last comment right now, from heaven. Yes, heaven, where the dead come alive and have a great time laughing at us all, mere mortals, stupid people, fretting over nothing, right? Tell me, are we endlessly, over the long haul, fretting over trivia? You'll tell me when I see you, which I hope and pray is a fucking long, long time from now. I don't miss you *that* much. This whole thing scares the hell out of me. As for the book that most influenced you, let's let that hang for a while. We'll come back to that.

We had great conversations, you said during our last good-bye. We did, we did. Except when you wanted to talk too.

I know, you can't help it. I'm funny. But indeed we did, profoundly deep ones in our shallow age: we talked about everything, about ideas, yes, but they could bore us if disconnected from people. Boy, did we talk about people, about who we are, about what motivates us, about Beaufort, our country, our society, friends, enemies, your stupid relationship with

The Citadel, your stupid relationships with everyone, even your relationships with old friends like Freddie who you hadn't seen in forty years. All played, even until the end, a prominent role in your mind.

Truth is all that mattered to you, which I found sometimes a pain in the ass. But we discovered that ignorance is not bliss, that what you don't know *can* hurt you, and that sometimes you had to do unto others *before* they did unto you. And though we created our own reality, that reality made us both a bit paranoid. God, did we hate critics of all types. Unless we were doing the criticizing, which we did all the time.

We visited Dachau in the summer of '68, when we assured ourselves with great authority—our own—that we'd change the world. Your conclusion: people were basically evil. Mine: no, their leaders were, but people were generally basically good. We had no idea, back then, our views were affected not so much by Dachau but by the way we felt about our fathers.

Your life has been as painful as it has been joyful. I know that. Back then I didn't believe you, when you talked about your father. No one did. Because you lied all the time, hell, you began lying for a living. Pat's exaggerating, like always, I told everyone. Until you painfully and relentlessly simultaneously sacrificed, discovered, and realized yourself with the truth, the only way you could do it, publicly, through your art, and when you did, you saved and warmed the hearts of the lives of so many people—yes, eventually, even your father's, the Great Santini's. You taught your father to love. Let me correct that. He always loved you, the only way life would let him, the only way he knew how. But you taught him to love *with* love, with humor, with warmth and tenderness. Pat, you taught your *father* to love. Your *father*. The Great Santini. And you think *he* was a war hero? He was, but you, Pat, became his. You had to, it was a matter of survival, and you did it with relentless love. You made him *see*. You made us all see, Pat, and what you and I discovered was that indeed we were both wrong, after Dachau, weren't we? The history of the world, all the emotions of every human being who ever lived, is in the heart and soul of each of us. Not either good or bad, but good and bad, and thank God for that. To look the other way, to deny, that is what makes us evil. The truth does liberate.

Let us return now to your study, your library, in

Atlanta, where we are talking with Pat Dickey about "character." The most important book of your young life?

Standing right there in front of me, third shelf down. Remember?

Lives of the Saints.

Subtitle: "The Autobiography of Bernie Schein."

Come on, you know that was funny. You can never keep a straight face with me. No one can. Right?

Your mom's love poured out of you your entire life. And the love of so many . . . I think, Pat, in all honesty, you are a saint. A shithead sometimes, but overall, a saint.

I love you, Pat. My heart, my soul, forever.

God's getting a kick out of you now, probably even more so as you tell Him stories about me. Please, resist that urge. I can hear Him now: *"When's Bernie coming, Pat? We need Bernie here!"*

Please explain that patience is needed here, Pat. That no, we don't need Bernie, not for a long, long, long time, thank you. And don't encourage Him just to piss me off.

I speak now to you, family, friends, admirers:

Pat asked me, knowing what was coming, to "take care of everybody." He loved so much, so expansively, which is why he was loved so much. He cared so much. He cared for us all, but of course, no one did he care for like his beloved Sandra, his truly beautiful daughters, so beautiful, in every way. Jessica, Melissa, Megan, and Susannah. He was so proud of you. When he was sick in the hospital and back at home and I was entertaining everyone with my formidable wit, your girls thought: *Oh, good, he's enjoying Bernie's humor so much,* but that wasn't entirely accurate. He was enjoying *your* enjoying my humor. While you were enjoying me, looking at me, he was enjoying you, looking at you. He loved so much. And like you, I love him so much. Pat will always be with us, inside us. And I promise you, as I promised him, I will take care of you. In fact, I can assure you, I will probably be a monotonous pain in the ass because even though it no doubt leaves you cringing in despair, it reassures him and makes him happy. So, up yours.

Kathy, Tim, Mike, Jim, Carol . . . I'm here, and I'm here for you to take me out to dinner as often as you like. Too bad we no longer have his credit card, but, hey, Mike just sold a house. What a brother is Pat, what a brother. I adore all of you, all of you. You're the best, far better, I used to tell him, than he was. He liked that.

I want to close by saying to everyone whose heart he has touched, whose soul he has comforted, and whose mind he has expanded, to all he has understood, inspired, and loved through words and his actions, to all his family, friends, and readers . . .

You have been in the presence of greatness, you have been in the presence of one who *dared* to be great.

Pat, you will live forever in our hearts, souls, minds. And I pray we are worthy to live now in yours . . .

He was a great artist—a great writer, a great teacher, a great friend—because he was a great audience. Writing, teaching, being a good friend is truly listening, turning your attention on a person so vividly it expands their image and vision of themselves. He made *me* feel great, not that I didn't already. Still, that's what love is, isn't it?

Eternally, I love you, Pat, always and forever, wherever you are, my beautiful, beautiful friend. I'm with you, my friend, inside you, of you, your heart, your soul, as you are with and in mine. Forever.

The Great Conroy

||||||||||||

An Homage to a Southern Literary Giant
and a Prince of a Guy

RICK BRAGG

✠

SOUTHERN LIVING, MAY 2016

He left the message every few months, the same message, word for word.

"Bragg? This is Conroy. It is now obvious that it is up to me to keep this dying friendship alive. You do not write. You do not call. But I am willing to carry this burden all by myself. It is a tragedy. Ours could have been a father-son relationship, but you rejected that. And now it is all up to me, to keep this dying [bleep, bleep, bleepity, bleeping] friendship from fading away . . ."

And then there would be a second or so of silence, before:

"I love you, son."

That part always sounded real.

I would always call back, immediately, but the voice mail just told me it was full, always full. I would learn, over decades, that it was full because I was not the only writer or friend he had adopted, or even the only one he left that same message of mock disappointment and feigned regret. But now and then I would actually be there when he called, and we would talk an hour or two about writers and language and why I should love my mother, and he would always, always tell me he had read my latest book, and how he was proud of me.

Then he would tell me how he did not mind that I had neglected our friendship and that his broad shoulders could carry the weight of my indifference, and the phone would go dead.

My God, I will miss that.

Pat Conroy died on the edge of spring. I won't try to add anything to the gilded language said over him; those who have read him know of the elegance there. I just know he was different from others at the top of this craft, different in his generosity. He was a champion, even for those who pretended not to need one.

Some two decades ago, when my first book was just months from publication, he wound up with a bound galley and actually read it all, and sent a message to my publisher with his thoughts. We call such endorsements, inelegantly, "blurbs." This was the best blurb ever written, lustrous and—now that I have had twenty years to consider it—undeserved.

But a thousand people since have told me they read it because he told them to, and quote the last line of that blurb to me: "I wept when the book ended . . . and I sent flowers to his mother."

But it was what happened, months later, that mattered most. He and his soon-to-be wife, the fine writer Cassandra King, came to visit my mother in Alabama, and brought her half a German chocolate cake. (My mother was too kind to ask what happened to the other half.) As he left, he offered to take my mother and elderly aunts home with him. "I'll cook for you," he said. He told me later he was impressed by my big brother, and my sister-in-law.

He looked in their faces and saw the utter absence of Old South pretension, and fell in love with that, too, a little bit.

As he left, I knew I was now only the second most popular writer in our home; *The Water Is Wide* is my mother's favorite book. Because of him, we see the good in Santini, and know that any man, no matter how wounded or damaged, can be a prince of tides. We will miss the words he had still to write.

We will miss a damn sight more than that.

Eulogy

||||||||||||||

DELIVERED BY JUDGE ALEX SANDERS*

MARCH 8, 2016
ST PETER'S CATHOLIC CHURCH, BEAUFORT,
SOUTH CAROLINA

Monsignor Cellini, Reverend Father Mac-Neil: Thank you for allowing me to speak today in St. Peter's Church. The Spanish philosopher George Santayana said that those who cannot remember history are condemned to repeat it. I have always thought whoever heard that quote is condemned to repeat it. Kipling said the same thing:

---

* Alex Sanders is a former president of the College of Charleston and a former chief judge of the South Carolina Court of Appeals.

"If history were written as stories," he said, "nobody would forget it."

Donald Patrick Conroy, born on October 26, 1945, was the best storyteller of our time—very possibly any time. We will never forget Donald Patrick Conroy.

He came to live in South Carolina on orders of the United States Marine Corps. In 1961, his father, Colonel Donald Conroy, a Marine aviator who went by the nickname of the Great Santini—perhaps you've heard of him—received orders to report to the air station in Beaufort, South Carolina. Pat was sixteen years old and received this news with dread. He had been to ten schools in eleven years and Beaufort High School would become his third high school.

When his mother drove her seven children into Beaufort County, none of them knew that they were driving toward his literary destiny and the reason all of you are here at this funeral today.

As they crossed the Whale Branch Bridge, he caught his first glimpse of the tidal marshes of the Lowcountry. That vision remained with him all of his life, and he was a marsh-haunted boy from that moment in time. Remember the first sighting of the marsh in the opening frames of the movie *The Prince of Tides*, and remember how Barbra Streisand praises the inexpressible beauty of the landscape. Of course, those were Pat Conroy's words. Both the book and the movie are love songs to South Carolina.

His mother, Peg, died of cancer. She is buried in the National Cemetery in Beaufort, beside Colonel Conroy. Pat supported nothing more strongly than the Hollings Cancer Center at MUSC.

He and The Citadel eventually kissed and made up and became great friends after a rocky relationship following publication of *The Lords of Discipline*. The Citadel has promised to stop using his books as kindling to heat the barracks.

Pat told me that The Citadel was one of the big reasons he loved South Carolina and the Lowcountry. While other writers of his generation were going to fraternity or sorority parties, he spent his four college years reading during Evening Study Period. He became a member of the Dock Street Theatre, the Charleston Ballet, and the Symphony. He learned about the beauty and charm of cities by studying Charleston and Beaufort.

Thirty years ago he wrote these words: "My wound is geography. It is also my anchorage, my port of call," the opening words of *The Prince of Tides*. He told me he didn't know where those words came from or why a fictional character named Tom Wingo was saying them. But he knew at that moment his third novel had begun.

These further words would soon follow:

I would take you to the marsh on a spring day, flush the great blue heron from its silent occupation. Scatter marsh hens as we sink to our knees in mud, open an oyster with a pocket knife, and feed it to you from the shell and say, "There. That taste. That's the taste of my childhood." I would say "Breathe deeply," and you would breathe and remember that smell for the rest of your life. That bold aroma of the tidal marsh, exquisite and sensual, the smell of the South in heat, a smell like new milk and spilled wine, all perfumed with sea water.

Through his eloquent words, he took us to that magical and unique place on earth.

His was a turbulent personality, a complex mixture of joy and despair, but through it all, great love. He loved books and independent bookstores, especially the Old New York Bookshop. Imagine that. He loved his friends, his brothers and sisters, his children and stepchildren, his grandchildren, his legion of readers, who hung on his every word and were enchanted by his characters, the atmosphere of the South Carolina Lowcountry, and his stories—always his stories.

But he loved no one more than Sandra, his steadfast wife, Cassandra King. She smoothed out the rough places for him and calmed the turbulence of his life. She loved him unconditionally, as he loved her. She brought him peace at last.

Pat Conroy may have come to live among us involuntarily, but he stayed among us by choice and enriched us all for more than fifty years. Many of us saw ourselves reflected in his published words.

Some of us he entertained grandly. Others of us he outraged greatly. To all of us, he gave a rare gift. He came to us from afar, like Faulkner and like Wolfe. But I respectfully suggest, in ways more real and more loving than either of them, that he gave to us the opportunity, in the phrase of Burns, "to see ourselves as others see us." For this alone, we should be forever grateful to Pat Conroy, our very own prince of tides.

"Good-night, sweet prince. May flights of angels sing thee to thy rest." *Hamlet*, Act V, Scene 2.

Man wonders but God decides

When to kill the Prince of Tides.

Please visit patconroyliterarycenter.org.

A living tribute to Pat Conroy's memory.

Acknowledgments

||||||||||||||

BY CASSANDRA KING

So many devoted friends morphed into worker bees to make this book happen when I was in no condition to do much of anything after Pat's illness and death. Although I can never adequately thank you, please know I am eternally grateful for your support and dedication to this project, born of shared grief but produced with tremendous love. On Pat's behalf, I am deeply grateful to the following: Mihai Radulescu, Pat's Prince of Romania, who had not only the vision for this book but also the willingness to see it through; Marly Rusoff, his extraordinary agent, advocate, and friend; Nan Talese, high priestess of the publishing world, Pat's Maxwell Perkins; Todd Doughty of Doubleday, who is always there for us as he was for Pat; Maggie Schein, the Conroys' way-overqualified assistant; and Margaret Evans, editorial assistant and researcher, steadfast through it all.

Special thanks to the board of directors of the Pat Conroy Literary Center, who are working to keep his spirit of generosity and his memory alive for generations to come.

And to the family: Carol; Mike and Jean; Kathy and Bobby Harvey; Jim and Janice; Tim and Terrye; Tom Conroy; Jessica, Bill, Stella, and Elise; Melissa, Jay, Lila, and Wester; Megan, Molly, Jack, and Katie; Susannah; Willie, Laura, and Baby-face Harvey; Rachel, Andy, and baby Kefonta; Michael Conroy; Barbara Conroy; the Harper boys; Gillespies; and Uncle Ed, Aunt Carol, and Conroy cousins.

Jim, Liz, Alessandra, and Alina Ray; Jason, Liz, Sophia, Henry, Anna Jane, and Harper Ray; Jacob, Brenda, Lucas, and Olivia Ray; Tyler; Michael, Brooke, Amelia, Isabella, and Caiden Ray; Rebecca and Reggie Schuler; Eric, Kyle, Matt, Elliot Schuler and their families; Uncle Rex; the Floozy cousins; and Will and Alayna Hare.

To our dear friends, whom Pat called the essentials: Janis and Wendell Owens, Bernie and Martha Schein, Aaron and Nancy Schein, Jonathan Hannah, Scott and Susan Graber, John Warley, Mike Jones, Pat Dinkler, Mina Trulow, Cliff and Cynthia Graubart, Ann Rivers Siddons, Terry and Tommie Kay, Sallie and Charlie Duell, Susu and Pug Ravenel, Alex and Zoe Sanders, Zoe Caroline and the boys, Judy and Henry Goldman, Dot and Peter Frank, Katherine and Brandon Clark, Kathie and Roy Bennett, Ellen Malphrus and Andy Fishkind, Patti Henry, Mary Alice Monroe, Marjory Wentworth, Ann Torrago, Hope Bach, Gay Talese, Carolyn Krupp, Eddie Birnbrey, Rachel Perling, Tricia Shannon, Ron and Ann Rash, Jim Landon, George Lanier, Ann and Claude Sullivan, Kathy and George Manning, Beverly Howell, Keturah Paulk, John Jeffers, Claire Simpson, Gregg and Mary Wilson Smith, Dot and Walt Gnann Jr., Wilson McIntosh, Jonathan and Lorene Haupt, Theresa Miller, Bill and Loretta Cobb, Tom and Carol Harris, Liz and Christian Sherbert, Lucius and Daryl Laffitte, Mike and Pat Roberts, Wendell and Florence Minor, Melinda and Jackson Marlette, and the Same Sweet Girls.

Finally, in memory of Nancy Jane King, Elton King, Tim Belk, Heyward Siddons, Milbry Gnann, Doug Marlette, Julia Randel, Eugene Norris, Kate Brockman, Hammond Smith, Jane Lefco, Nugent "The Boo" Courvoisie, Julian Bach, Jay Harbeck, and Barbara Warley.

ABOUT THE AUTHOR

PAT CONROY wrote eleven books, including *The Water Is Wide, The Great Santini, The Lords of Discipline, The Prince of Tides, Beach Music, My Losing Season, South of Broad,* and *The Death of Santini* before his death in March 2016 at the age of seventy. For more information, please visit patconroy literarycenter.org.

patconroy.com

ABOUT THE TYPE

This book was set in Goudy Old Style, a typeface designed by Frederic William Goudy (1865–1947). Goudy began his career as a bookkeeper, but devoted the rest of his life to the pursuit of "recognized quality" in a printing type.

Goudy Old Style was produced in 1914 and was an instant bestseller for the foundry. It has generous curves and smooth, even color. It is regarded as one of Goudy's finest achievements.